ONE MAN'S SEARCH FOR THE DIVINE

Andre Serge Patenaude

ONE MAN'S SEARCH FOR THE DIVINE
Copyright © 2021 by Andre Patenaude

All rights reserved. No part of this book may be reproduced in any form or by any electronic or mechanical means, including information storage and retrieval systems, without permission in writing from the publisher and author, except by reviewers, who may quote brief passages in a review.

This publication contains the opinions and ideas of its author. It is intended to provide helpful and informative material on the subjects addressed in the publication. The authors and publisher specically disclaim all responsibility for any liability, loss, or risk, personal or otherwise, which is incurred as a consequence directly or indirectly, of the use and application of any of the contents of this book.

ISBN: 978-1-955531-12-2 [Paperback Edition]
        978-1-955531-13-9 [eBook Edition]

Dedicated

to my wife Joyce who has been

my muse since we first met

and

to my beloved teacher Prem Rawat also

known as Maharaji who saved my life

ACKNOWLEDGMENTS

I am grateful to Michelle, my daughter, for her encouragement. Whenever I mentioned the book I was writing she rallied me on; to my sisters Dianne, Huguette and Monica for their support and feedback; to my brother in law, Dick Nelson and his wife Sandi, who listened to me often about what I was writing; to all those friends who would suggest that I write a book after hearing my stories. And, I'm eternally greatful to my wife, Joyce, for signing me up for a writing class and having faith in me and being emotionally supportive in my process. She truly has been my muse since we first met.

INTRODUCTION

It has taken me over ten years to write this book. Many times I have put it aside, sometimes for years, but the impulse to tell my story has never let up so when it would become strong enough I would give in and write maybe a paragraph here, maybe a correction there and sometimes whole chapters would flow as if the words were writing themselves. At times as I was writing, I would have thoughts like: "Nobody is going to be interested in your story;" or "This is very boring just forget about it;" or "What are people going to think of you once they read this." The shameful feelings I often had while writing would compel me to stop writing. Shame had been a significant part of my life for many years. It was a big part of my Catholic indoctrination and my mother often used shame to control me. Shame was also as a result of being sexually violated at the age of seven. Sometimes the shame came from the memories of the many people that I have hurt and disappointed. Sometimes it was the interest or enthusiasm that gave out.

Nevertheless the impulse to share parts of my life with the world has never let up.

It is clear to me that my Master teacher, Prem Rawat (also known by the honorary title of Maharaji), saved me from ultimate self-destruction. It is also clear to me that he was the answer to my prayers for help because as you will read in my story he came along at the perfect time.

My children were also instrumental in changing the course of my life. My beautiful daughter, Michelle, who entered my life at the age of twenty-three, was a God-send.

Sometimes we have a prescient glimpse into the future and we can see where a particular road that we embark on will end up. I know that the announcement of my daughters' arrival into my life would save me from a potentially lethal path. The direction of my life had already started to go down a dark tunnel when I saw the possibility of her arrival. Alcohol and sex had already ensconced itself into my brain as a regular compulsion. Even with the limited awareness I had as a young twenty-something I could sense sociopathic sensations. I never would have referred to those feelings in such a pathological way, but I knew that those impulses were pretty dark. So the arrival of my daughter saved me from a life that could have wound up as criminal.

Another major shift of direction in my life came along with the announcement of the birth of my son, Alexander. When I first learned about his arrival a familiar voice inside said: "It's time for you to get your manhood together." It changed my path from that of an adult adolescent male to manhood or from the adolescent "Prince" to the adult "King" as Michael Gurian explains in his book The Prince and The King. I'm very grateful to the creator for sending me these wonderful angels.

And lastly I'm eternally grateful to my wife, Joyce, for her cherishing, loving, caring, supportive and forgiving nature. She has been supportive of me since we first met. She saw the gifts as a healer that I had way before I did and encouraged and at times pushed me to recognize my gifts when I often dismissed myself with statements of "no big deal." I often say that the Universe knows who we are and will bring to us or guide us to the events or people that will help us to evolve and my wife has been a big part of my evolution.

There have been many people on my evolutionary path that have made a difference and to all of them I'm eternally grateful.

PART I
THE SEARCH BEGINS

It was about seven in the evening on a Monday in May 1972 and generally a slow night at the German restaurant where I was working as a waiter. I was serving a family, a young girl of about nine and her brother age about eleven and their parents when the phone rang at the manager's station. For some strange reason I had a sense that it was for me when I saw the manager answer the phone. He then put the call on hold, walked towards me and said: "André, emergency call for you." He took care of my table and I picked up the phone. Cindy was on the other end crying.

"My mother found your poem," she said.

"Yeah, so?"

"So she showed it to my father."

"What happened?"

"He asked me about it and I told him that it was none of his business and then he beat me up."

"He beat you up? Why did he beat you up?"

"I told him that the poem came from you and that we were just friends. Then he called me a whore and a liar and smacked me across the face and I'm sitting here with a fat lip and a swollen cheek."

"What do you want me to do?"

"The minister is here and they all want to talk to you. Can you come over?"

"Who's they?"

"My father, my mother and the minister. I need for you to come over now."

1

ONE MAN'S SEARCH FOR THE DIVINE

"Okay. I'll be there in ten minutes."

"Thanks."

When I got off the phone I told the manager that I had an emergency and asked if he could give my table to another waiter and I left.

Driving to Cindy's place and thinking about the crisis I was about to confront took me back ten years to another crisis when I was living in New York. My partying days had come to a screeching halt a few days after my twenty-second birthday when Carol, a fellow airline reservations agent and who had been my girlfriend for about six months, called me from her hometown in Castlewood, South Dakota to tell me that she was pregnant and "what was I going to do about it." She was upset and angry and it made it pretty irksome for me to talk to her, let alone go and see her. Suddenly, her father took the phone and said:"Hi, I'm Bill, Carol's father. How you doin?"

"Well, right now I don't know. I'm a little shocked."

"Yeah, I can imagine. How would you feel about coming down and helping us sort this out?"

"I'll do whatever I can."

"Good. I already feel good about talking to you."

"I feel good about talking to you too."

Carol got back on the phone and said: "What are you going to do?"

"I'll call you back tomorrow morning."

I called my boss at the office and told him what was going on and asked for a few days leave, which he granted and along with the weekend I had four days off. I made airline reservations for the following afternoon and called Carol back and told her to pick me up on the evening flight into Watertown, South Dakota about 20 miles from Castlewood. She sounded surprised when I told her I'd be there the following night. She agreed to pick me up at the airport.

Something inside of me stirred when I found out that Carol was pregnant. It was like the soul getting ready to come into this world through this baby was making direct contact with me and saying: "I'm coming to help you change the course of your life."

2

Andre Patenaude

There was a sensation of warmth and tingling through my entire body as I contemplated this child coming into my life. There was also a feeling of acceptance and unconditional love (at the time I would not have called it that). I was ready to meet this new being and the challenge that came with it.

The following evening I stepped off the plane in Watertown and was met by Carol and her mother and father. Carol and her mother were cold and distant, but her father greeted me warmly just as he had on the phone. He made eye contact with me and I relaxed immediately. We drove the twenty miles in silence. Castlewood is a small farming community of about six hundred. Probably very much like other small farming communities in the mid-west. They do have stop signs which most of the residents ignore but no traffic signals. It was curious for me to see that there was a church for just about every Protestant denomination and one Catholic church.

Dinner was waiting along with Carol's three younger brothers and the family pet, a Mexican Chihuahua whom I teased long enough for him to declare me a permanent enemy. The meal was quite pleasant and typical of a farming community: roast beef and mashed potatoes with gravy and some vegetables. Apple pie and coffee for dessert of course. The meal was mostly spent in silence. The boys were in school so homework was an immediate focus after dinner. It was announced that the next day we would all meet with the family's Lutheran minister. Everyone was a bit stressed and tired so we all went to bed early. I slept on the couch in the living room.

The next day Carol, her mother and father and I met with the local Lutheran pastor.

Religion was an immediate issue with the women and being a Catholic was not met with much favor. Discussion as to what to do became quite emotional. Carol's doctor in New York had told her that she'd never be able to carry a baby to full term and if she did he couldn't guarantee that she would survive the birth. She had a damaged heart valve due to a bout with rheumatic fever when she was a child. Her New York doctor told her to get an abortion. The family doctor in South Dakota, who had been taking care of her since she had been a little girl had no doubt that she could sustain the pregnancy and see it through delivery. So abortion was out and the pregnancy was in. The subject of marriage entered into the picture.

Religion now became an even bigger issue. Carol's mother, grandmother and aunts wanted us to get married in the Lutheran Church. It was important to the family and their image and especially to please grandma. "Grandma will die if Carol marries in the Catholic Church, don't ever marry a Catholic," was a familiar refrain Carol had heard as she grew up. For two days there were endless talks of having the birth and

3

ONE MAN'S SEARCH FOR THE DIVINE

giving up the baby for adoption to getting married in another town. Carol's father Bill, took me aside and told me that he would support whatever decision we arrived at. It seemed as though he was my only ally in this family. Yes Carol's pregnancy was a source of shame but in a town of six hundred people not only did everyone suspect what was going on but it would not have been uncommon.

During these few days I met grandma. Grandma was of German descent and a staunch Methodist. She was thin with gray hair and wore glasses and probably always looked like a grandmother. Every time I saw her she looked like she had just been crying. According to everyone she was a severe and unbending matriarch and everyone was afraid of crossing her except for her husband who's harshest words to her was: "If you don't like it, you can lump it!" It seemed to me that her demeanor was a way of keeping people at a distance and affection like hugs were few and far between. Having grown up with French habits of greeting, I always approached grandma with a huge hug and a kiss on both cheeks which always seem to catch her off balance melting away her defenses. She morphed into a shy teenager whenever I greeted her and I played to the family's concepts of my French heritage. I was never afraid of her I even liked the old lady. Bill, Carol's father, however, seemed to have an antagonistic if not at times hostile relationship with grandma.

I asked Bill about the hostility between him and grandma. "There are so many reasons why I don't like the old lady," he said. "But the main reason is the way she meddles into my personal life and crosses boundaries and nobody calls her on it except myself and the family gets upset with me when I do." "Don't upset grandma she has a bad heart," they all tell me. " For example, I enjoy a drink on occasion Sometimes I'll go to the local pub and have a beer or a vodka and tonic. By the time I get home from the pub, the whole town knows about it and I'm perceived as a drunk according to the old lady. The only way to keep booze in the house is to hide it because grandma would at times walk the two blocks to visit and if no one were home, she would let herself in, because we don't lock our doors and scrounge around looking for bottles of booze in the cupboard, the closets, the pantry and the basement. If she found a bottle of my favorite vodka, she would pour it out and refill it with water. Nothing was ever said, but the usual suspect pointed to grandma." For some reason Bill and I cracked up with laughter over this story. It was so absurd.

It had been less than two years since I had left home and my strong childhood Catholic beliefs were still very fresh. Even though my church attendance had dropped significantly since I had left home, getting married in any church, but the Catholic Church was not an option. After all I had never stepped inside a Protestant church. A Catholic marrying in a Protestant church would not be acceptable to God and I would be excommunicated on the spot from the Catholic Church and the

4

Communion of Saints. I would never again benefit from the graces of all the saints and my soul would suffer eternal damnation if I died immediately after excommunication. Also, God would let me know how displeased he was with me for marrying a non-Catholic by putting a curse on my children in the form of some kind of birth defect. In my family we had proof of God's wrath if you crossed Him by marrying a non-Catholic. One of my mother's sisters married a Protestant who never converted to Catholicism. They had eight children and one boy was born with a club foot and another, a girl, was mentally challenged. So no way was I getting married in a Protestant church. It was different for the Protestants. They would not merit hell if they married in a Catholic Church. It seemed to me that the decision was clear. I had a greater risk if I married in her church.

Thankfully their Lutheran minister was a liberal guy and he persuaded the whole family to agree to marry in my church. We set the date for December 15, 1962 and we went to the Watertown Catholic church and petitioned for the marriage ceremony. Carol would have to agree to instructions in the beliefs of the Catholic Church and also agree to raise the child Catholic. It was that or no marriage and she reluctantly agreed. Grandma was not going to die after all and the rest of the women would just have to suck it up. The following day I returned to New York and was told that my transfer to Miami had come through and I was to report for work at the Miami International Airport on the first of December.

A few days after I arrived in Miami I found a small one-bedroom apartment in Miami Springs just a few blocks from the Catholic Church. I had been told by the priest who was marrying us in Watertown that I needed to contact a priest in my community and make some arrangements with him for some pre-marital counseling. A few days after I moved in I made contact with the priest at the church.

My office manager wasn't very pleased when I asked for some days off to get married. He said: "It's a hell of a time to be getting married during our busy season. I won't give you the time off." Fortunately my work schedule was set up so that the weekend I was to get married, I had Thursday through Sunday off.

On Thursday, the 13th of December I arrived in Watertown and Carol's father met me at the airport and told me that Carol was in the hospital. It was nothing serious, just an increased high heartbeat from too much excitement. The day before, the priest who had planned to marry us had called her and told her that, in good conscience, he could not marry us because of some of the answers I had given to the priest in Miami. He told Carol that pregnancy was not a valid reason for marriage. When the priest in Miami had asked me why I was getting married I told him that my fiancée was pregnant. He asked me if I would marry her if she wasn't pregnant

5

ONE MAN'S SEARCH FOR THE DIVINE

and I answered in good conscience: "no." And that was the truth. Decisions had to be made and it seemed to me that I was the one holding the wild card. A moment of clarity from deep within myself surfaced and I made the decision to marry outside the Catholic Church. Not having my parents who were staunch Catholics or any other member of my family attend made the decision making a lot easier.

The tension was noticeable when we arrived at Carol's house. Everyone was in an agitated state of suspense. So far I had kept my decision to myself. When Carol told me about the Catholic priest's decision to not marry us I told her that I was willing to get married anyway and that this was my life and no priest or church were going to tell me what to do. There was such a sense of empowerment and freedom as I verbalized that statement. It seemed as though all this constricted energy coming from fear in my body was released all at once. It was a great high.

We immediately made arrangements to have the ceremony take place Saturday morning at the Lutheran Church with the family pastor presiding. Friday night we had a short rehearsal and that was my first time ever in a protestant church. It was scary, but I suffered through it.

During the ceremony, I started to get a bit nauseous. I wasn't sure if I was going to pass out or be turned into stone for the great sin I was committing. Thankfully it was a short ceremony and we walked down the aisle towards the entrance doors. Once I stepped outside, I fully expected to be struck by lightning. My paranoia about being struck by lightning lasted for several months. God was going to get me one way or another. He'll strike when I least expect it.

The wedding reception was at Carol's house. Friends and family had brought many delightful dishes, including a home made wedding cake and of course coffee. We toasted with coffee. No booze allowed, grandma's footprint on our wedding. Sometime during the reception, Bill, Carol's father sneaked me down to the basement and poured me a double shot of Vodka. When the coast was clear we both sneaked back upstairs to rejoin the celebration. That night Carol and I shared a bed for the first time since we split up.

The following day we returned to Miami.

Ten years later, in Minneapolis, I was on my way to encounter another crisis, which would again become radically life changing. Cindy had been my baby-sitter. She was almost six feet tall, pretty with long curly black hair that came down past her shoulders.

Andre Patenaude

Her blue eyes sparkled when she smiled. At eighteen, her body was solid with ample breasts. Whenever I saw her she smiled and life for her was carefree. She smoked pot as did all her friends and I often bought a baggie from her or one of her friends. Cindy often invited me to parties that her friends gave and was always proud to introduce me as her friend although I was fourteen years older than her. Often at these parties I also got stoned with her while she and her friends introduced me to the latest music.

The poem that was the source of contention had to do with a weekend I had spent with Cindy. It was the Easter weekend when my wife and daughter had gone to South Dakota as I had given the excuse that the restaurant needed me for a very busy Easter Sunday and I stayed behind. Cindy and I had gone to a friend's cabin in the woods across the Mississippi River in Wisconsin that was the subject of the poem I had written for her.

A friend had given me two tablets of psilocybin and Cindy and I decided to trip out together at the cabin. We brought a portable stereo record player because Cindy wanted me to hear some new music that had just come out. It was Led Zeppelin IV.

Three miles before the cabin we stopped at a roadside cafe and ordered an orange juice and swallowed the tablets of psilocybin. We then drove to the cabin and on the way we smoked a joint. Trees surrounded the cabin. Adjacent to it there was a horse ranch.

There was a small river that flowed fifteen feet past one side of the cabin and continued South about 300 feet then curved around and went back toward the other side of the cabin on the far side of the driveway. You could take an inner tube and start on one side of the cabin, float down the river, and get off on the other side fifteen minutes or so later. A beautiful pastoral scene just waiting for a poem to be written.

After we set up the stereo player and lit the fireplace the psilocybin started to peak. Led Zeppelin IV was playing and I sat back, closed my eyes and let my body absorb the sound of the music. When Stairway To Heaven came on, I was already hallucinating and saw myself walking across the universe. I was both very large and at the same time very small. I seemed large at first and could easily have held the planets in my hands butcompared to the rest of the Universe, I was quite small. As I was walking through space to the beat of the music a friend popped out of the right side of my body and with the next beat another friend popped out of the left side of my body. With every beat following, afriend would pop out of each side of my body until

7

a huge circle of hundreds of friends was formed and I was the hub in the center of the circle. My friends were all walking hand in hand to the beat of the music and I was in the center.

The walk through space was exhilarating. I was free of all fear and inhibitions. All of my fears and thoughts of people not liking me were gone. All the impulses of avoiding contact with others were gone. The paranoid feelings I had regarding family, friends, and society were gone. I no longer felt like a victim. In its place was a feeling of exhilaration, liberation, clarity, power, well-beingness and vibrancy.

At some point, my friends in the circle started to retreat back into each other and when the circle was half gone I started to panic. A soft and kind voice in my head said: "You were okay by yourself before your friends came and you'll be okay again after they're gone." I knew that the voice was telling me the truth and I relaxed. The process of retreating continued and as the last one disappeared and I was alone again, I heard: "...and she's buy uy ing a stair air way to heaven."

I was so blown away by that vision that I can remember it today many years later just as if it had been a few minutes ago. I was overwhelmed with amazement by the vision I had. I knew that visions did not come in a pill. What was it in me that created this cosmic vision and in total synchronicity with the music? Needless to say, the message was a foreshadowing of things to come. I knew that I had tapped into something that would be with me for the rest of my life. Yes, I had friends and I had internalized them and they were okay with me and I with them. And I also had come to the realization in this vision that I could be alone without being lonely.

There is one other significant event that took place at the cabin. Under the influence of psilocybin, boundaries were pretty fuzzy and I felt so grateful to Cindy for introducing me to this music that I came on to her and she gently pushed me away. She said: "I like you and might even love you because of who you are but I thought you knew that I'm into girls. André, I'm a lesbian I don't do guys, but if I did do guys I'd want to do you and I'm flattered that you would come on to me".

I was more surprised than shocked. In a way I was pleased with being rebuffed by Cindy because it surely would have changed the tone of our relationship if we had been sexual. I could now experience Cindy as a person. Something that was always difficult for me with women. I had started to admit that I saw women as sexual objects for my personal enjoyment and emotional intimacy had been foreign to me.

Driving to Cindy's house while trying to figure out what I had written in the poem that so incensed her mother and father was annoying. Upon arriving at her house I felt an inner calmness and strength rising from my guts. I knew that I would be okay. I was ready to deal with whatever consequences would come up. Cindy's mother answered the door. She appeared to be ten years older than her middle forties. She gave the impression of someone who had been emotionally battered. She had a serious and frightened expression on her face and her eyes were red and puffy from crying while avoiding eye contact with me and looked at the floor when I walked in. Cindy was on the living room couch curled up in a fetal position. When she got up to greet me I could see her swollen lip and her left cheek had swollen to such an extent that her left eye was closed. She told me how humiliated she felt and apologized for bringing me into "this mess." She then introduced me to the minister and her father. The room was completely filled with tension.

We all sat down around the coffee table in the living room. With some anger in her voice, Cindy said: "My mother was snooping through my things and found the beautiful poem you had given me. She showed it to my dad today when he came home from work.

He asked me who had written it and when I told him that it was none of his business and that they had no business snooping through my room. That's when he beat me up."

"Where is the poem," I asked?

The mother said: "I threw it into the fireplace and burned it after I showed it to my husband. It was disgusting." Now I would never find out what I wrote.

The father said: "Mary Jane was mentioned in the poem. Is that a reference to marijuana?"

"Yes," I said.

"Have you smoked marijuana with Cindy"?

"Yes."

"Do you really think it's okay for you to give her pot?"

Before I could answer Cindy jumped in and said: "I've been smoking pot since I was fourteen years old and drinking since I was much younger. All the kids I hang out with do it. It's no big deal."

"Personally," I said, "I don't see much difference between pot and alcohol. I have the same attitude towards both, that is, taken in moderation it's not troublesome. Cindy is eighteen and old enough to experiment."

ONE MAN'S SEARCH FOR THE DIVINE

"Isn't it against the law?"

"Yes, but it's a stupid law and physically abusing your kids is also against the law."

Cindy expressed to everyone that she felt violated and betrayed by her mother and father and apologized again for getting me into this "mess."

Then the minister said: "Are you having an affair with Cindy?"

"No," I said with relief. I remembered how gracefully Cindy had refused my sexual advances and I was now grateful that she had. I assumed a total air of innocence during the evening. As far as I was concerned the bad guys were the parents.

The minister asked me: "How would you feel if this was your daughter and she was involved in a similar situation?"

"If my daughter was to meet a man similar to myself at the age of eighteen and he treated her and loved her the way I treated and loved Cindy, I would be happy for her."

I wasn't sure how this would go over, but by now Cindy's parents were feeling so guilty and ashamed of their behavior that I thought I'd rub it in a little bit. "And I'd be grateful to that man for being so kind to her."

My answer seemed to have deflated their antagonism.

Then the father asked: "Does your wife know about your relationship with Cindy"?

"She loves and appreciates Cindy as our babysitter but she doesn't know about our trip to the cabin. And she doesn't know about the poem and I have no desire to tell her about it."

"What do you think she would say if she found out?"

"I don't know."

"I have a good mind to call her and tell her."

"Do what you want. I don't have any control over that."

"You know I can have you dismissed from teaching for what you did."

"Maybe you can and I don't have any control over that either but do what you feel

10

you need to do."

"I want you out of this house right now and don't ever contact Cindy again and if you do I'll make big trouble for you sonny boy."

I left the house and went home with a sense that my life as I had known it would change I just didn't know how. When I got home, Carol said: "Your home early." I made up an excuse about it being slow at the restaurant which was true but it had nothing to do with me being home early. It always amazed me that Carol believed my lies, something I had been doing my whole marriage.

The next day Cindy called me and said: "Don't worry about my father. I told him that if he ever touched me again or tried to make trouble for you, I would tell my mother about his affair. I told him that I would tell the authorities that he had sexually violated me since I was fourteen until I put a stop to it a year ago. You should have seen the look on his face when I told him. He had no idea that I knew about his affair. He denied it at first but when I told him the name of the women he was having an affair with he turned pale and begged me to never tell my mother."

Cindy was her cheerful self again and shortly after school let out, she moved in with her girlfriend lover and was quite happy. She even invited me to have dinner at their house so that I could meet her lesbian lover.

The next day I got a call to do substitute teaching at Washburn high school just walking distance from my house. As had been my habit for about six months I ingested some blotter acid and downed it with orange juice. I liked subbing at this school because Cindy was a student there and the students were hip and I knew quite a few of them.

I checked in at the school office for my assignment, I was given instructions for my class which had been called in by the full time teacher. It was a senior English Lit. Class.

I went to the classroom and as was my custom I greeted the students by the class doorway as they arrived. When the bell rang for the beginning of class I heard someone down the hall yell out: "Please hold the door open." It was a student running down the hallway a little disheveled. I waited for him and after he had entered the room I heard in a loud and stern voice behind me say: "What do you think your doing?" I turned around and it was the vice-principal.

"What do you mean what am I doing?"

ONE MAN'S SEARCH FOR THE DIVINE

"I mean, what are you doing letting that student into class without a late slip."

"He wasn't late," I said.

"Yes he was and I want you to send him to the office for a late slip."

"Why should I do that?"

"Because those are the rules."

"I'm not going to do that." I walked into class and shut the door as I heard him say: "I'm going to report you."

My heart was beating a little fast as I asked one of the students to take attendance. To me, the vice-principal's behavior was absurd. It was also a behavior that I had observed many times from school administrators. In the past I conceded to their requests. This was the first time that I defied their authority. It just seemed to me that sending this studentdown to get a late slip was unkind and asking for disciplinary problems. By now I had stopped identifying with the system. I identified more with the students. Whenever I thought about becoming a full time teacher, I inherently knew that I would never make it. After attendance was taken I gave the students the assignment from their homeroom teacher and I parked myself at the desk and began reading The Book sub-titled The Taboo Against Knowing Who You Are by Alan Watts. Boy was I in the right mood for this book. Earlier I had read a book by Paul Goodman titled Growing Up Absurd.

That book helped me look at life with a new perspective. As radical as Goodman's book was,it made a great deal of sense to me. I was a few pages into Watts's book when I sensed someone standing in front of my desk. It was one of the female students standing there with her right hand shoulder high. I said: "Yes."

"May I go to the bathroom please?"

This wasn't the first time that I had heard a request like this in a high school. This time though the absurdity of that request struck me and I said: "No" and returned to my book and waited. I immediately felt the attention of the rest of the class focus on the exchange between this student and myself.

"Why not?" She asked.

"Didn't you just ask me permission to do something?"

"Yes."

"Then doesn't that give me the right to grant you permission or deny it?"

"Well, yes."

"Well, I chose to deny it."

She was getting a little bit embarrassed so I said: "Look. I'm suppose to know where you are so just tell me where you're going. Don't ask me. O.K.?"

"I'm going to the bathroom. All right?" she asked.

"No it's not all right. You're still asking me permission."

Then she said angrily: "In case you want to know where I am, I'm going to the bathroom."

"Congratulations. Good for you. You got it." And I applauded.

When the student returned to class, I stationed myself on a stool in front of the class.

"Can anybody tell me what was going on with the exchange I had with Mary (not real name)?"

"You were giving her a hard time," said a girl in the back of the room

"You humiliated her," said another girl.

"She was merely following the rules and you put her down," said a male student.

"You were rude and insensitive," said another.

"You should follow the rules," one of the boys said.

"Yeah, you have to have order," another boy said.

"You were just trying to teach her a lesson," said the boy with hair down to his shoulders.

"What lesson do you think I was trying to teach her?"

"You were trying to teach her that it was O.K. for her to go pee without having to ask your permission," he said.

ONE MAN'S SEARCH FOR THE DIVINE

"Close. Anyone else?"

After a few seconds of silence, I said: "The lesson that I was trying to teach is: If you give someone else the power to give you permission to do something, you then take a risk.

A big risk sometimes. You give me power to control your life. Can you see that? Most of you are old enough to vote for the president of the United States, the president of the most powerful country in the world and you have to ask me permission to go pee. Some of you guys are old enough to be sent off to Vietnam and kill or get killed yourself and you have to ask me permission to go to the bathroom? Doesn't that sound a little bit absurd to you?"

"Well if we all got up to go to the bathroom at the same time there would be chaos," one student said.

"Yeah. You can't just do what you want," said another.

"Do you really think that you would all have the urge to go to the bathroom at the same time? And if you did you'd all be standing in line waiting your turn. My daughter is nine years old and she doesn't ask me permission to go to the bathroom. I get paid to be here and I don't have to report to anybody to go to the bathroom."

"Your promoting chaos and disruptive behavior," a boy said with an anxious expression on his face. His body language was quite rigid and although he was seventeen maybe eighteen, he looked older. He didn't sound like a teenager. He sounded like a parent. He sounded older than me although I was fifteen years older. I got that impression not only from him but also from others in the class.

"Mary, I apologize to you if I humiliated you. Would you share with me and the class what was going on with you?"

"Well, I was a bit confused because I always got permission before. No teacher ever said 'no' before. Then I got scared. Then I got angry. I thought you were trying to embarrass me."

"How did you feel when you finally got it and told me where you were going."

"I felt really good."

"Did you feel empowered?"

14

Andre Patenaude

"What does that mean?"

"Did you feel strong?"

"Yes."

"Compare that with the feeling that you had when you were standing there with your hand up asking me permission to go to the bathroom."

"What do you mean?"

"What were you feeling when you were asking me permission?"

"I felt foolish."

"Did you feel strong then or weak?"

"I felt weak."

"Now, let me ask all of you another question. Why do you come to school?"

"To get a diploma," some students said in unison.

"Because we have to," others said.

"I don't see anyone standing behind you with a gun forcing you to be here. How many of you got stoned on your way here this morning?"

"What do you mean?" asked one of the boys.

"I know that some of you walk in here stoned in the morning. I'm just curious about why you get stoned knowing that you're going to be in school all day."

The male student with shoulder length hair answered: "Cause it's awfully boring in this school and getting stoned gets me high and I can tolerate this school a bit better."

I said: "As I see it there are about eighteen hundred students here and the curriculum allows for about twenty some odd courses that you can interest yourselves in and its difficult for me to imagine that you are all interested in the same twenty things. So again I'm asking you why do you come to school?"

"To get a diploma," one student said.

ONE MAN'S SEARCH FOR THE DIVINE

"Why do you need a diploma?"

So I can go to college," said another.

"Why do you want to go to college?"

"So I can get a good job and make a lot of money," the same student said.

"Why do you want to make a lot of money?"

"So we can buy things." They said in unison.

"Do you think that buying things will make you happy? I have a college diploma. Do you call this a good job and do you think I make a lot of money? I'm saying all this to you because it's time that you took your life into your own hands and went with it. It's time for you to examine what we've been teaching you and perhaps determine that the answers for your life are not necessarily here in school or the books that we tell you to read."

Just then the bell rang and they all left the room in a hurry. What I was saying to the class I was also saying to myself. I had seen myself trying to fit into some kind of mold that was totally foreign to me. At thirty-two I still didn't know what I wanted to do with my life but I knew that what I was doing wasn't it.

As the next class started I gave them the same assignment and went back to reading my book. After about fifteen minutes a male student came to the desk and announced that he was going to the bathroom. News spreads really fast.

The next day when I returned to the same school to substitute for the same teacher, I was met at the classroom door by the vice-principal with a note that the downtown office was dismissing me and that to be reinstated I'd have to have an interview with one of the administrators downtown. I left the school and went to the downtown office to see whatthis was all about.

At my interview with the school administrator I was told that a parent of one of the students from the previous day's class had called the principal of the school and accused me of encouraging the students to quit school. I was asked to explain what had happened the previous day and I shared about the exchange with the students. The administrator smiled and told me that he understood and asked me to "tone it down a little," and he reinstated me as an active substitute teacher.

When I went home that day and while I waited for my daughter to come home from school and for my wife to come home from work, I thought about the absurdity of my life. I had thought about it many times but this time it was more like I was feeling it in my psyche. I had been totally hooked to all my addictions: sugar, alcohol, pot, sex, porn, lies and psychedelics and they were taking precedence over everything. I had come to Minneapolis to study to be a Lutheran minister at the age of twenty-seven and within a few months of starting my studies, I'm smoking pot; cheating on my wife and sleeping with co-eds; partying with my teenage classmates and doing psychedelics. At the same time I had a full load of studies, holding down a part-time waiter job and doing a poor job of being a father and even a worse husband.

Looking back over my life it seemed as though I had been plagued by some dark forces that I didn't comprehend or admit to myself. I was out of control and I was beginning to see it. I had been out of control for quite a few years, probably since I left home. At the time, addicts were perceived as those who were on hard drugs like heroin or cocaine so it had been difficult to see myself as an addict. Getting high was the only way I dealt with despair. I had been numb most of my life. I did psychedelics to be able to feel. I liked myself when I was high. I felt that childlike innocence and playfulness. When I didn't get a substitute teaching gig, I would do some acid and go to the park and play with the kids. Not like an adult playing with the kids but like a big kid playing with the other kids. There was one park near our house that had a hill to one side and I would go to the top and make sure that there was no dog poop on the grass and roll down the hill sideways. When the younger kids would see me doing that, they also would try to imitate me and some of them would ask me to roll down with them so I would cuddle them around my body and roll down with them to the bottom and it was fun. Today I imagine that it would be viewed with some suspicion, but it was all innocent. Sometimes I would do acid and hop a bus in the front of my house and ride it all the way back and watch the passengers as they entered and left. It was like a silent play on wheels. There would be such an empathic connection with the passengers. I would imagine a story for each one.

At the same time that all this is going on I felt very alone and isolated even invisible. Nobody knew what was going on with me. My family had no clue because I had been so good at pretending to be whatever they had wanted me to be. I was like a chameleon, blending in so that I could feel safe. Pretending to be somebody I'm not wasn't working anymore but at the same time I had no clue who I was.

Many times I had thought about ending it all. I was so afraid to tell anybody even my therapist about my suicidal thoughts because I was afraid to be committed to an institution and I really didn't trust the people in the white coats. Hell I didn't

ONE MAN'S SEARCH FOR THE DIVINE

trust anybody. Trusting anything in this world was too dangerous. I could not trust my parents, my church, my government, my teachers, my wife, my therapist and even myself. The only person in this world I trusted was my daughter.

It seemed like each year things just got worse and worse. The bottom line at the end of the year was always the same: zero and more disappointment. We worked to pay the bills and there was no end in sight. There was just more stuff around the house. I had a deep longing for something and didn't know what it was and sometimes there was a deep pain in my solar plexus and when I paid attention to that, what I felt was an emptiness that seemed like an infinite precipice. When I would share my feelings with people I would often be told to come down to earth and "be like us" and "don't be so idealistic." That never helped me. I didn't seem to have any control over these feelings. It wasn't like I was creating them. My feelings of despair often would happen after I had been on psychedelics or pot. My future looked like a perpetual dead-end. I knew that I couldn't do psychedelics the rest of my life.

My father had passed away the year before at age fifty-nine of leukemia and burned out from working for a living as a mechanic and my father in-law died six months earlier not able to recover from open heart surgery. He was also fifty-nine and burned out. At the time of his death, I remember thinking to myself that there really was no good reason for him to come back. It was no mystery to me that he didn't come back. I never felt that he was appreciated for who he was and coming back was to experience more of the same stuff that put him on the operating table to start with. These two deaths made a profound impact on me and on my thoughts about my own future. I didn't think I would even make it to forty let alone fifty-nine.

My friends and family couldn't figure out what was "wrong with me." To them I had everything one needs to be happy: a beautiful wife, a wonderful child, a good job, a nice home, great friends and everything I needed to make me happy. So externally there really was nothing to make me depressed and suicidal. I should just get my act together, stop complaining and enjoy my life. Take my head out of the clouds. But I was dying inside and I had no idea what was going on and neither did anyone else. These feelings were not new. They had been there ever since I was a child. The way I dealt with those feelings as a child was with sugar, then alcohol and when my body was ready, masturbation.

At the age of thirty-two, the only comfort I felt came from satisfying my urges and the books that I read. Most of the books I read were referred to me by what I called my mini gurus, my young college friends. The authors I read gave me hope. They talked about the loneliness and feelings of alienation that we can go through. They talked about how we live in a state of illusion. Illusion. That was a new concept

18

for me. Everything was an illusion, Maya, the unreal. Some of these teachings were confusing. They also talked about a resolution to my dilemma by going into Nirvana or Samadhi or God consciousness and as I read these books something inside would long to meet these wise men so that they could teach me how I could achieve what they knew but then, I would learn that all these authors were dead. It made me even more depressed and hopeless.

I WANT SOMEONE WHO CAN HELP ME. SOMEONE LIVING. It was like I had three parallel lives: one life was that of a husband and father and everything which that implied; another was as a closet addict, and the third was searching for some kind relief that was more transcendent.

For as long as I could remember life was painful and each year the intensity of the pain increased. I numbed myself with more and more drugs and alcohol. If the future was to be more and more of the same or even worse, then why keep on going I would say to myself. I remembered very much identifying with a song in 1969 by Peggy Lee called: Is That All There Is and I used to listen to it over and over again and thinking that someone knows exactly how I feel. And for me if what I was experiencing in life was more and more of the same then it wasn't worth it. I knew that there were people that liked me and some even loved me but it was never enough or fulfilling enough for me. I realized in those moments that if the whole world loved me it still wouldn't be enough.

Material things or money didn't impress me either. As a teenager I would fantasize having a lot of money and what I would buy with that money. Sometimes I would take that fantasy to such a place that I knew that whatever amount of money I would accumulate it would never be enough. I would always want more. If I had ten million, I would want twenty and if I had twenty, I would want fifty million and on and on. I also knew that material things would not satisfy me. By now I was used to longing for something and getting it and feeling disappointed that the thing that I wanted and got did not do for me what was promised by the seller or what I had imagined I would feel once Igot that thing. I already had a houseful of stuff and it was just that, stuff.

One time when I was living in Anchorage, Alaska I used to walk by a stereo store and once in a while I'd go in and listen to some of their stereos. The sound always impressed me when I was in the store. So I saved enough money to buy the same stereo that I had been listening to and when I brought it home, installed it and played it, I felt betrayed because it didn't seem to sound like the one in the store nor did I have the same feeling as I had in the store. That incident left a deep impression. So it seemed to me that there were so many promises that fell short.

ONE MAN'S SEARCH FOR THE DIVINE

It was the same way with religion, big promises of salvation and a dead-end up ahead. I had also assumed that having a higher education, which so many people advocated as the way to enlightenment . That was also a big hype. And here I was thirty-two years old with a wife and a ten-year-old daughter, a college education, a failed attempt at a religious ministry, a failed attempt at being an educator with a bleak future ahead of me.

And to make matters even bleaker, I'm totally at the mercy of my addictions. The hallucinogens I was ingesting almost on a daily basis now were creating a lot of confusion. I didn't know what was real anymore. I felt a deep sense of alienation and isolation. I was often panic stricken and had difficulty being on time for anything. Leaving my wife and daughter was not a pleasant thought but staying seemed even more unpleasant, especially for my family. I was totally out of control and I knew it.

At the same time that all of this confusion and delirium was happening, I was also aware of a deep longing for something to fulfill me, something that would make me feel complete. I didn't even know how to explain it to myself let alone ex-plain it to anyone else. Even my therapist seemed to be oblivious to what was going on with me. To be honest I never gave him much information that would help him help me. I knew on some strange level that there were answers somewhere, I just didn't know where or what theywere. Where to turn? Where to go? Was I losing touch with reality? Since being a teenager people often told me that I was a dreamer, an idealist. People would tell me that what I was looking for didn't exist. I felt trapped, at a dead end and outraged and verymuch in despair and feeling a bit insane.

I called Joel, a friend of mine who seemed successful and happy. He seemed to be in a solid marriage with his wife Gina. They were both entertainers. He was a concert pianist and sang opera and she was an opera singer. Whenever I was with them I felt so solid and appreciated. I often envied what they had not only in their relationship but also professionally. They seemed quite secure and I was void of any security whatsoever.

Fortunately he was there and I started telling him about how unhappy I was and how lonely I felt and how depressed I was. He listened patiently and lovingly. Then he said: "André you shared this with me before and it seems like you're still stuck in the same place. If I were you I would go a little bit deeper then you've already gone and find out what this is all about for you. Let yourself feel at the deepest level no matter how painful it is or how scary it is and perhaps you'll find some answers there." It wasn't the answer that I wanted to hear but I knew that he was right on and that he had taken a risk by his response.

What resonated for me was "no matter how painful or how scary." Up until now I had been avoiding the pain and the fear by getting stoned or drunk or popping acid. Within a few hours, I could see that I couldn't go on any longer with my life the way it was. It was obvious to me that my life was totally absurd. I had known that it was absurd on an intellectual level but now the realization of the absurdity of my life hit me very hard.

That evening after my daughter went to bed I told my wife that I was taking a leave of absence for a year. I said: "I don't know what I'm looking for and whatever it is I'm not finding it here with you and Michelle. I know that you both love me and I wish that were enough but it's not. So this afternoon I realized that my life had not been my own since probably before I started school as a boy. And if I don't claim my life back now no one will give it back to me. No one will give me permission to do what I need to do. I know that this is a great risk that I'm taking and that it will cause some difficulty for you and our daughter but it will be even more difficult on you both if I stay. What is going on with me is not your fault and if you're not here when I come back in a year, I'm willing to risk that and with no grudges." As the saying goes: "It's not you, it's me." My wife was a good and loyal person. Being in control was important to her especially with a husband who was often out of control. She had tried pot with me once or twice, but it didn't do it for her. Learning that her husband was using LSD on a regular basis made her eel very insecure. We were living in two different worlds. She went off to work every day and I either had a teaching assignment or I hung out at home or at a friend's house stoned. She deserved better than this. And with my daughter what could I point to and say: "go for it." What was going on in my life that was so ingratiating and passionate that

I could say: "Go for it." Lord knows that I tried a lot of different things and went for it, but everything I tried was a dead-end.

And if you really wanted to get me mad you could tell me: "God loves you." What does it matter if God loves me if I'm so shut down that I can't feel love but only depression. Or maybe the wound in my heart had been so widely torn that all the love I was receiving was falling into this huge rupture in my soul. I never understood what the ache and void in my heart was all about, but the pain and despair had gotten less tolerable each day.

The most difficult part about the decision to split up was telling my daughter. The next day when I told her about my decision, she said: "Daddy I know what you're looking for.

ONE MAN'S SEARCH FOR THE DIVINE

You see, life is like a puzzle and you have a missing piece in your puzzle and that's what you're looking for." I wasn't surprised by her answer because she always came up with some wise saying, but I was astounded by her clarity. She was exactly right. There always seemed to be something missing in my life and whatever I ventured into was a way to find the missing piece to my puzzle. The missing piece wasn't marriage, kids, job, career, drugs, and money. Things, none of that is ever fulfilling. The missing piece was me and I didn't even know it.

The following Saturday we went to see our therapist with the news that I was leaving. At the end of the session, he said to me: " I know that you have to do what you have to do, but you're wife might not be here when you get back." "I know, but that's a risk I have to take," I said. I was out of the house a week later.

I was visiting Robert Baker, a friend and therapist, who pretty much knew about my circumstances and as we were talking I noticed a book on the shelf just above his left shoulder. The title was Be Here Now by Ram Dass. This had been a book on my recommended reading list.

Actually the only book that had not been crossed off my list.

"Robert, can I see that book," I asked?" "Sure. It doesn't belong to me. As a matter of fact I don't know whom it belongs to. It seems to be floating from one person to the other. You can take it with you if you like." I took it with me and started reading it with great passion.

I was fascinated to read about Ram Dass' journey because it was very similar to my search. I could never tell anybody what I was searching for because I wasn't sure and to tell people that I was searching for God seemed a bit too religious for me and I had had enough of religion. There was one statement that Ram Dass made in the book that relieved me of a great deal of anxiety and that was " You don't find the Guru, the Teacher, he finds you when you're ready." I remember thinking to myself "Then help me get ready."

It fit with everything else I had been reading that captivated my attention. I need a teacher. I need someone who can show me what to do with my life because here I was thirty-two years old and I still didn't know what to do with my life. Whatever I tried that promised some kind of fulfillment I pursued with with great passion and I kept hitting a dead end. And then I'd be faced with extreme depression and feelings of inadequacy. I constantly felt like a fish out of water. Was there something wrong with me that I wasn't fitting into society with a plan, with some contribution? Couldn't people see that I was lost? Wasn't my college education supposed to show me what to do with my life? Did I miss something along the way? Somebody or something please help me.

And whom could I turn to for guidance? Did I dare tell the men with the white coats that I was crazy? Would they know what was wrong with me and how to treat me? I intuitively knew that I couldn't trust the establishment to know what was happening with me. Authority was something that I had learned to trust implicitly as a child and as an adult had learned to distrust. If I didn't know what I needed in my life to feel fulfilled how was anyone else going to know? If my Ph.D. teachers in college had not succeeded with me in finding fulfillment then maybe I was being "unrealistic" and I should just put my nose to the grindstone and work and support my family and retire someday and die and forget about fulfillment. But somehow the Universe or God responded to my inner silent pleas for help and gave me some hope through Be Here now. I declared this book my new bible. If I were to carry only one book on my journey this would be the one.

Carol had been working for Western Airlines for about four years now and decided that she also needed a change. It had never been her decision to live in Minneapolis, it had been mine so she applied for a transfer to the Denver, Colorado office and got a transfer within weeks.

That summer I stayed here and there with different friends. I went to work one day at the German restaurant and there was a sign on the front door: "Closed. Will reopen under new management." It seemed that life as I knew it was changing daily. I drove out to the horse ranch in Wisconsin next to the cabin where Cindy and I had experienced mescaline. I had befriended the owner and so I asked if he would take me on as a worker for room and board. He was thrilled to have me work for him. He had four daughters and although they were all very helpful and what seemed to me very knowledgeable around horses, he missed having another man around. I spent the rest of that summer working on the ranch from morning to dusk and it was a perfect healing experience for me. Before my daughter left for Denver she had an opportunity to spend about a week on the ranch with me.

In the mornings I walked about a mile and a half out to the fields and gathered up the horses. The horses were always at the furthest section of the ranch from the stables. I would take a piece of bale twine and put it in my back pocket so that the horses wouldn't see it and get spooked (a trick the owner had shown me). If they saw me walking towards them with a twine or rope in my hand they would move away and I would have to chase them all over the place until I caught my assigned horse. I would put the twine around his neck, gently jump up on his back and drive the herd to the stables on bareback. The child in me was constantly present when I was with

ONE MAN'S SEARCH FOR THE DIVINE

the horses. Riding the herd back to the stables at a full gallop with the wind in my hair amongst the one hundred or so horses, the sound of their hooves pounding the ground, the dirt they were kicking up would sometimes hit my body and watching their manes flowing with their gallop was exhilarating.

After I got the horses back to the corral we would then select which horses we would saddle up for the riders that day. I learned to sneakily corner the horses and rope them and lead them into the stable. I also learned to saddle them up and put bridles on them. There were many tricks I had learned to sometimes "outsmart" the horse. Sometimes the horse would fill up his belly with air and let the air out after the saddle was on and then the saddle would slide to the bottom of the horse when the rider would try to get on. So I Learned to notice these little horse tricks and gently kick them in the belly with my knee so that I could put on the saddle properly. When people arrived to ride around ten AM myboss would interview them to see how much riding they had done and he would usually cut that in half and then determine which horse they could ride. The guys always wanted the biggest and fastest horse. But Al the owner knew his horses and always chose a horse appropriate for that person's experience. Often he would give a small horse to a macho guy knowing that although small, the horse was frisky. Often then the response would be met with "I want a bigger horse." Then Al would give them a bigger but very mellow and slow horse . Al would wink at me and we'd both laugh about it later. If some guy gave him lip about having a particular horse that Al didn't want him to ride, he would just tell them to go somewhere else. The women would often just ask for the mellowest horse, the more gentle the better. It wasn't always the smaller horse that was gentle; we had mares that were big but very mellow.

Then I'd take them to the trail. On this trail there was always an open area where they could gallop and usually the guys would just go for it and sometimes so would the girls. But if they took their horses back covered with sweat, Al would have them walk the horse until it cooled off.

Within about two weeks of working on the ranch I had developed a wonderful relationship with Al and his family. They often would invite me for dinner and always inquired about my needs. Did I have enough to eat? Was I comfortable in the bunkhouse?

Boy I could not have designed my summer better. Every night I slept in the bunkhouse and loved it. The mornings were always met with enthusiasm. Sometimes my friends from Minneapolis would come out and ride. Sometimes Cindy would come out by herself and we would go riding together or with a group. I eventually realized that this ranch had been a wonderful gift that the Universe had arranged for me and it was so healing.

The end of the summer came and the horses started growing winter coats. I made one trip to another ranch with Al about a hundred miles further north. He took a truck loaded with horses and I took a truck loaded with hay and that was my final adventure for the summer. I felt that I had healed from my emotional separation from my wife and daughter and was ready to start substitute teaching again. I found a furnished apartment a block from Ausburg College and began accepting calls for subbing.

The Renaissance Fair was still going on during Labor Day weekend and I decided to spend the weekend with friends at the Fair who had a booth selling antiques. After hours when the fair was closed was the most interesting time. The campfires would light up the night and the air was rich with smells of barbecues and pot. The bottles of wine and the ever-present joint were passed around and musicians were strumming their guitars and singing their songs. One particular artist by the name of Shawn Phillips was popular at the time and a musician and his girlfriend were singing one of Shawn's songs. As I complimented them on their music, the man said: "Would you like to go see Shawn Phillips tomorrow at the Marathon II concert?" "I don't have any money," I said. "The ticket is free if you want to go," he said. I took the ticket and thanked him. And as I walked away he said: "Here's a four way capsule of organic mescaline for the concert."

The concert was an all day concert at the University of Minnesota football stadium and featuring Albert King, Shawn Philips and Loggins and Messina. I had no idea what was waiting for me on that day. I called Ruthie, a co-ed, from Augsburg whom I had graduated with for a ride to the stadium since I didn't want to hassle with parking and she agreed.

When Ruthie dropped me off at the stadium she handed me a joint of Columbian and said: "Here, this will help you get started." I wasn't aware of it at the time, but I was going through a major identity crisis. I had been a married man for ten years and a father for most of those years. I was thirty-two years old with long hair and a beard and although I might have looked like one of the hippies in the audience, my internal identity was not congruent with my external appearance. With the effect of the Columbian marijuana on my brain, I became extremely paranoid.

I was sure that every hippie there was looking at me and judging me as a phony. I was so overwhelmed with paranoia that I couldn't enjoy the music. So I did the next best thing and swallowed half the capsule of organic mescaline.

ONE MAN'S SEARCH FOR THE DIVINE

As the effect of the mescaline started to be felt, Albert King took the stage and my body started to respond to his music and the tightness and the paranoia which I had been feeling for about two hours started to release. After a couple of songs, I was jumping and yelling with everyone else. By that time, about 22,000 people were in the stadium. WhenAlbert King finished his set I was quite impressed by the whole experience and since Shawn Phillips was next I told myself: "Shawn, you'd better be good because I'm pretty impressed already."

The mescaline I had taken was already starting to peak, so by the time Shawn Phillips got to the microphone, the energy in the stadium seemed so focused and connected that I was already pretty open and impressed. The instant Shawn started singing he had us in the palms of his hands. He started with the first song from his Second Contribution album and the 22,000 fans were right with him to the music and the beat. At one time when I wasn't sure what to do with the music, I closed my eyes and saw geometric patterns of color and the patterns changed with each beat and then the patterns disappeared and only a rainbow of colors remained. Then as the words "…. and it's brighter than the sunlight, and it's purer than the moonlight, and it's drawing me toward it like a moth out of thenight…" from "Song for Sagittarians," the rainbow of colors closed like a Japanese fan and I saw a golden light that felt so loving that I wanted to merge with it. At that point, my mind came in and said: "Open your eyes, you're dying." I opened my eyes immediately and I was euphoric. A strong impulse to run down to the stage and kiss Shawn's feet was vetoed when I saw the tight security around the stage.

At one time we were all clapping to the music and Shawn said: "At the count of three, stop clapping." I thought to myself right. How are you going to get 22,000 stoners to all stop clapping at the same time." Then he started to count: "one." And by the time he got to "two" the only doubts I had was whether or not I could stop clapping. And then he said: "Three." I stopped clapping and so had everyone else. Silence. There had been this loud music and 22,000 people clapping and then silence. It was the most noticeable quiet I had ever heard. Then it was "one, two, and three," and the music started again and everybody just went nuts. Was it possible that we could all be that connected and yet we were? Needless to say, the rest of the concert was a very high experience. Instead of calling for a ride home after the concert I walked the three miles home extremely energized. As I walked home and thought about the feeling I felt from the golden light I had seen, I started to remember reading about inner light in religious scriptures and other transcendent literature. The next day I bought three of Shawn's albums and whenever I got depressed I would play his albums.

Andre Patenaude

One day, in late September, when I didn't get a call for a teaching assignment, I went to the Augsburg cafeteria for a cup of coffee and possibly some familiar company. My friend John was there and he was accompanied by a beautiful young brunette named Elizabeth. I joined them and after some light chit chat I said: "I've got some hashish that a friend gave me recently would you like to come to my place to try some?" So of course they agreed. We got stoned and eventually I took John home. Before I left I told Elizabeth that I'd be glad to give her a massage when I got back if she wanted to wait.

When I got back Elizabeth was still there so I gave her a massage, which eventually led to sex of course.

Within a few days, Elizabeth became a frequent guest in my apartment. She was young, nineteen, beautiful and vivacious with a sense of humor that made me chuckle often. The sex was always passionate and we were stoned most of the time when we were together.

I had already resumed substitute teaching when Elizabeth came into my life. I also got a waiter job in the new French restaurant in the IDS building in downtown Minneapolis. I still had a ponytail at the time and was told by the Maitre' d that I'd have to get a decent haircut. So I bought a wig to wear over my long hair until the day that I couldn't find it and got a haircut.

One day in November I got a letter from Dianne, my baby sister who was now living in San Antonio, Texas, telling me that she and her boyfriend and his sister had just opened a free school for adolescent homeless kids. She wanted me to join them in this new benevolent project. So I called her to get more details and asked if Elizabeth was included and of course she was. I inquired from my other sister, Huguette, about the situation with Dianne in San Antonio and she was doubtful that what she was doing was legit based on her recent visits. However I wanted to believe so badly what Dianne was telling me that I put Huguette's doubts in the back of my mind.

Elizabeth and I discussed the invitation for a few days and since neither of us had any major commitments in Minneapolis, we decided to go on this adventure. Shortly after Thanksgiving we hitched up a small trailer behind the Plymouth and headed south. Just before leaving I talked to my friend Ken about my move and he recommended that we stop in Ames, Iowa on the way down and visit his sister Mary who is a psychic. He gave me her phone number and called her in advance to introduce us.

ONE MAN'S SEARCH FOR THE DIVINE

When we arrived in Ames I called Mary and she said that Ken had called her and that she was expecting us. So we drove over to her house and had dinner with her and her family. We were invited to spend the night so Elizabeth went to bed early and I stayed up to talk with Mary. Mary is like an earth mother, very maternal and nurturing, which was apparent in the way that she related to her children. Her voice was always calm and soothing. In spite of no makeup, she had rosy cheeks with long salt and pepper hair. She was breast-feeding her youngest at the time which added to her aura as earth mother.

"Mary" I said, "Ken tells me that you are a psychic and I was wondering what it is that you picked up from us and our trip to San Antonio." Mary replied: " Well before you arrived I contacted the spirits and they told me that you were not going to find what you are looking for in San Antonio but that you should go there regardless. And for Elizabeth, what I see is a balloon within a balloon and the inner balloon is expanding and eventually it will break through the outer balloon. The spirits also told me that they would be with you on this journey and to pay attention to them."

The next morning Mary had breakfast ready for us and had baked some extra muffins to take on our trip. We bid goodbye and left with a sense of guidance and protection.

The drive through Iowa was a bit boring at that time of the year and by night fall we were in Oklahoma and in some very dense fog. The temperature light on the instrument panel started flashing and we pulled off the highway and to a garage only to find out that the fan belt was broken and replacing it was a minor problem. After about an hour we were on the road again in some very dense fog. As we were driving along at about 35 miles an hour and listening to country music, the song Your So Vain came on and it was the first time either one of us had ever heard it. So it became our theme song on this trip. We spent the night in a cheap motel and the next day we headed for San Antonio.

When we arrived near San Antonio, I called my sister Dianne and told her where we were and she and Buddy, her boyfriend, drove out to meet us. When they arrived, Dianne jumped in the car with me and Elizabeth jumped in the car with Buddy and off we went to Jack in the Box for Tacos, French fries and Dr. Pepper. Of course, Dianne got me thoroughly stoned and Buddy and Elizabeth were pretty stoned by the time we got to Jack in the Box.

I had some doubts about the legitimacy of my sister's new interests. Were we already seeing the flakiness that we had been told about? But I guess I wanted to believe the possibility of this new open school project and that someone felt that

I could make a contribution that I put my doubts on hold. When we arrived at the school which was also a resident for the staff, we were shown the "projects" and "achievements" of the students. There was a painting of a lion that we were told was done by a student and that it would be turned into a poster which people could buy to "support these street kids." We were shown a wood working shop and an art studio. I guess all of the doubts that I was still harboring were still on the surface because I broke down crying with relief upon seeing all the good works of the school, staff and students. We were told that there were only about a half dozen students but that it was growing one student at a time.

The local TV media were scheduled to do specials on this new open school. After about a week pot was put on hold for a few days and the media came. Two local TV stations did a story on the school and as might be expected, donations started pouring in. After a few weeks, it occurred to me that things were not what they seemed on the surface. For one thing, most of the so-called achievements from the students were really borrowed from people outside the school to give the appearance of talented homeless kids being taken in and expressing their gifts in an open setting. Also, these homeless kids were not homeless after all but friends of the family who were used as pawns to give the impression of creative activity. The aroma of marijuana reeked in the air like burning incense. For Christmas LSD was given as gifts to the staff. Most of the week blew by under the influence of acid.

Whenever the owner of the building would come around to collect the rent, Buddy's sister, the administrator, would leave through the back door and they would make excuses for her and ask the owner to come back some other time. One time after she had disappeared and returned in her VW bug, the car was so filled with smoke that when she opened the door I was almost knocked over by a cloud of marijuana smoke. After seeing this scenario a couple of times the picture as to what was really happening started to become pretty clear. These people were pulling a scam.

They were trying to get money from some benefactors to keep the school going and live their drug lifestyle and it was a total con. If I hadn't been so stoned myself most of the time, I probably would have noticed something sooner. Elizabeth, who was a bit more coherent than the rest of us tried to warn me many times about what was happening especially when Buddy's sister tried to come on to me, which I was oblivious to. I was in denial big time. I just didn't want to believe that I had been misled. But eventually the dysfunction of the whole scene became more and more obvious not only to myself but to the owners and donors.

When it became clear that this was not what it appeared to be, Elizabeth and I moved out to a house near the Air Force base where the rents were reasonable

ONE MAN'S SEARCH FOR THE DIVINE

along with two other guys from New Hampshire who had also been conned into believing this story of the open school and tried to figure what our next move would be. Because of Elizabeth's talents as a seamstress we decided to make pillows out of some fabrics that she hadbrought with her from Minnesota and sell them at a local flea market. That lasted about two weeks because we could never sell enough pillows to make a living.

Between being stoned half the time and doing acid at other times and kind of existing a spaced out life we never got much done. The other two guys found a marijuana connection and sold pot to friends in New Hampshire, which they shipped via the Trailways bus line. Our funds were running out so Elizabeth cashed a 500 dollar bond that she had received for coming in first in the Junior Miss Minnesota pageant. One day during a sober moment I decided that I would cut my hair again and get a waiter job at a four star restaurant. After interviewing and getting hired at the Hilton four-star restaurant, I had to buy black pants and white shirt and black bow tie. Going back to work, as a waiter seemed like I was going backward in my life but at the time I thought that I had no other option.

My first day on the job was a Tuesday because they wanted me to start on a slow day. I arrived at the restaurant almost in an altered state. Lacking in enthusiasm and feeling ungrounded, I went to my assigned tables and did the customary wiping down of the silverware and wine glasses. The maitre'd gave me customers at two of my tables and I was so overwhelmed that I couldn't do anything right and after two hours and making many mistakes I realized that this again was another dead end and I quit. This was a first for me quitting a job after two hours. I could almost visualize my father turning over in his grave upon seeing his son being so irresponsible. Because if there was one thing myfather was, it was responsible. At the same time, I felt so freed up. In spite of being spaced out most of the time, I was clear enough to know what didn't work for me.

When I got home that night Elizabeth greeted me with some confusion and said: "We received a letter today from Mary, Ken's sister." The letter read: "Dear André and Elizabeth, when you left my home a few months ago I told you that I would be sending the Spirits with you and they've come back to tell me that you are not listening to them, so they've asked me if I would write to you. The Spirits told me to tell you two that you both have things to talk about that you are avoiding. They won't say what it is because you both know what the Spirits are talking about. They also told me to tell you that they are back with you now and for you to start to listen.

Andre Patenaude

We had a little dinner and then we got stoned and started to have sex in our bedroom. While we were fucking I had a strong sense that someone was in the room watching us. I said to Elizabeth: "

I can't continue because the hairs on the back of my head are standing up because it feels like someone is watching us." "I feel the same way," she said. The sense that there was someone, a presence in the room watching me was a feeling I had had many times since I was a kid. I had always interpreted this "presence" as the boogeyman. Someone my parents introduced me to when I was probably three or four so that they could control my behavior when they weren't around. As an adult, I often felt it in the basement of my house or in the attic or sometimes I would be lying in bed wide awake in the middle of the night and sense that it was under my bed or in the closet or in the hallway waiting for me and I would have to turn on all the lights just to go to the bathroom. In my home in Minneapolis, I had a pool table in the finished basement and I could never go and play pool by myself because, after a few minutes, I would start to sense that the boogeyman was there somewhere. He was never there when I was playing pool with friends only when I was alone. And of course I never told any body about this for fear of being labeled crazy or insane. We also kept a second refrigerator in the basement where I would stash my beer. One night after coming home from my waiter job, I smoked a joint and went down to the basement to get a beer and as I started coming up the stairs I could feel this boogey-man just a few steps behind me and I just ran up the stairs in a state of terror and slammed the door shut. Like I said I never discussed this with anyone not even my therapist. I didn't want to be committed to the "men in the white coats."

So here I was with Elizabeth, who also felt as though someone was watching us. I felt a bit less terrified since I wasn't alone. Maybe these are the spirits that Mary is talking about, we thought. Needless to say, continuing on with sex was not going to happen. So I sat up and said: "I don't know if you are real or just a projection of my imagination, but if you are real then you know that I'm having a hard time. And if you are trying to give me some guidance, it's too subtle and I'm too dense. So I'm going to go to sleep now and you come and show me in a dream what to do with my life because I have no idea what to do with it and I'm tired of the confusion and anxiety.

I had learned a few years back how to do lucid dreaming, so I was planning on using that technique as soon as I went to sleep. Within minutes, I was dreaming that I was standing inside the TWA building at Kennedy airport in New York. I wasn't sure what I was doing there, but I got the impression that it was to meet someone. Some of thewindows inside this building designed by Aero Saarinen go from the ground to the roof and as I was looking out the window onto the tarmac a huge airliner like I had never seen before taxied up to the gate in front of me. It had three cockpits.

31

ONE MAN'S SEARCH FOR THE DIVINE

A major one in the nose of the aircraft and one on each side of the nose. As I was mesmerized by this sight, two people walked over to me as though they knew me. One was an Indian looking man about twenty one about five foot ten, slim and very well dressed in a light beige business suit with a tie and wearing glasses. The other person was a young man of about twelve or thirteen who looked familiar. As this young man and I eyeballed each other I sensed a deep wisdom and mercy. Everything I had ever wanted to feel, I felt. I felt unconditionally loved and accepted. I felt a compassion and mercifulness with a no nonsense attitude. I got the impression that the younger of the two was in charge.

I started to walk towards where my transportation was and they started to walk at a pretty good pace in another direction. I ran after them and yelled, "what time is it?" There was no response and they continued at the same pace. I yelled again "what time is it?" This time they both stopped, turned around and looked at me. The non-verbal message was: "it doesn't matter because we are here now." And they turned around and resumed their pace. I threw myself on the floor and had a tantrum and beat my arms and legs on the floor of this terminal building and screamed out "I want to know what time it is." As I said before I was doing lucid dreaming and I'm watching myself throwing this tantrum and wondering what the hell was all that about because that is not my M/O. It also seemed that I felt safe enough to throw a tantrum without being shamed or criticized or judged.

They both stopped walking and turned around to look at me throwing a tantrum. The younger man eyeballed me, looked at his watch and eyeballed me again and said: "If you want to know what time it is, close your eyes and look inside." Again since I was lucid I thought to myself:

"I can trust this person" and in my dream I closed my eyes and went into another dream. In this other dream I found myself in a community of people who were calm, serene and peaceful. They spoke Sanskrit and I understood it. And I thought to myself: "I don't remember learning Sanskrit." Then someone handed me a stone tablet with Sanskrit written on it, which described my life at that time. When I got to the bottom of the tablet, the lines started to scroll and described my lives one by one accompanied by a holographic slide show.

After a few minutes, the slide show sped up and everything became a blur until I was in a scene in a house in a familiar neighborhood in Minneapolis. This was the first house my wife and I lived in when we moved from Anchorage. In the dream, it was wintertime and there was a fresh foot of snow on the ground. I was standing outside on the porch looking at the street when a red Volkswagen bug driven by a woman with a male passenger drove by going from left to right. She looked at me as she drove by and made an erratic u-turn and hit a telephone pole. The male passenger's door opened and the man fell out as though he was dead or knocked out.

The woman got out of the car and stared at me as she walked towards me. She had wild looking black hair and red lipstick over-covering her lips.

She also had a menacing look in her eyes, which scared the hell out of me so I ran inside the house and slam shut the door. I continued to observe her from the living room window and watched her come up the porch steps, open the door and enter the house. I was so freaked out that I wokeup. I shared my dream with Elizabeth and decided to go to sleep and deal with the dream the following day.

As I was waking the following day, the idea of "looking inside to know what time it is" seemed to me was more than just finding out the time. It was time to make some decisions that I had been avoiding. I told Elizabeth that I was going to go to the Lama Foundation in San Cristobal, New Mexico where the book Be Here Now was published. I thought that maybe they had some answers for me. In Ram Dass's book, he says: "You don't find the Guru, he finds you when you're ready." I didn't know if I was ready or not, but I was going to find out.

I gave Elizabeth the option of going with me. The message that I got when I did look inside was that this was to be a solemn journey. However, I was still attached to Elizabeth and not too enthusiastic about going alone. I decided to do the thousand mile journey by bike. I know. What was I thinking doing a thousand mile bicycle trip in the middle of February?

I put an ad in the paper to sell my car. About two days later a Mexican man and his kids came by to check out my 1967 Plymouth Belvedere. I sold it to him for $300 and included a tool chest in the trunk with my father's tools. I was rapidly getting rid of my possessions. The trailer of personal belongings I had left Minneapolis with a few months before would be too much of a burden to carry around.

After selling my car, Elizabeth and I went to a bicycle shop and we bought a ten speed bike for her. I already had a bike. We bought backpacks, bicycle tools, sleeping bags, and a pup tent. We also got a basket to put in front of the bike for our dog, Krishna. I didn't tell you about Krishna. At Christmas time, one of the kids at school brought us this small black dog as a gift. This bitch was like a miniature black lab, about four or five pounds. I liked the name Krishna from the chanting so that became her name. I had no idea what the name meant, but I liked the sound of it. Little did I know that on this journey: "Krishna come here," would happen hundreds of times.

ONE MAN'S SEARCH FOR THE DIVINE

On February 10, 1973 Elizabeth and I and Krishna took off on our thousand mile long journey to the Lama Foundation in San Cristobal, New Mexico. On the bike carrier over the back wheel, I had a pup tent in its original box with my sleeping bag on top of it. I had my backpack on my back with all of my earthly possessions. Mostly clothes and the book Be Here Now, which had become my new Bible. On the front of my bike, I had Krishna in a small straw basket with a small blanket for her comfort. Elizabeth also had a carrier on the back of her bike with her sleeping bag. She carried her backpack on her back. It must have been hilarious to anyone watching us trying to get on our bikes with our backpacks and with all this baggage over the back wheel. We took off with much fanfare from our friends and neighbors.

About a block and a half away, Krishna jumped out of the basket and ran off. This was not a good sign for our journey. We finally retrieved her and took off again. I guess she decided that jumping off at that height was not a good idea because she didn't do it again for a few miles. We headed for route 90 West. Once we got on the highway, it felt like the easiest trip in the world. We had a tailwind that pushed us along with our backpacks acting as sails. We had done about six or seven miles and rolling pretty fast when Krishna again decided that she didn't want to participate in this adventure and jumped out. Well, I tell you at the speed that I was going, she hit the ground and rolled about twenty feet. We both stopped and checked her out. She was a bit traumatized I think, but unhurt.

Now getting on and off a bike with a backpack on your back and the bike carrier loaded down is not the same as getting on and off when you're free of these accoutrements. Each time takes some maneuvering. I couldn't swing my leg over the seat because of the loaded up carrier. I had to tip the bike to the side and put my leg over the bike in that position. Once I was back on my bike, Elizabeth put Krishna back in the basket and we were on our way again.

We had planned to camp out the first night near Medina Lake. According to our road map, it was just a few miles north of Castroville. We turned off route 90 and took Ranch road a two-lane highway going north. By then my butt was starting to ache from the seat and when I looked back at Elizabeth, it looked like the initial enthusiasm for this adventure was already depleted. There was a part of me that was more and more pleased the more miserable she appeared. Although I wanted her with me I knew on a deeper level that this was to be a solemn journey for me and resented that she had taken me up on this trip. So here we are peddling on Ranch road with a head wind making every yard seem as though we were peddling uphill and we had just begun our thousand-mile adventure.

Andre Patenaude

We didn't make it to Medina Lake. The more I saw the pain in Elzabeth's face the more sorry I felt for her so I suggested that we just camp out in the woods near the road. That night we set up our tent for the first time had a snack and cuddled up under our combined sleeping bags and fell asleep.

The next morning we awoke still with sore butts, refreshed a headed for Castroville for breakfast just a few miles from our campsite. By the time we got there our butts were already asking for mercy. After breakfast, we headed out again on highway 90 towards Hondo, sixteen miles away. We had lunch there and took another break. After resting our butts we headed out again. When we got to Sabinal twenty miles further, we decided to call it a day. At this pace, our arrival at the Lama Foundation would probably be June or July.

We wanted to camp out someplace where it would be safe and legal so we went to the Sheriff's office and told the Sheriff about our plans and he suggested an empty lot at the end of town. My cover story this whole time was that I'm a high school teacher on sabbatical and writing a book about my travels. And though I had a beard and longer hairthan is acceptable in what I was warned was redneck country, being a high school teacher gave some legitimacy to my appearance and behavior. So Elizabeth and I biked to the end of town and found an empty lot. We felt good about having the Sheriff in our protection. As we were pitching our tent, he pulled up in his official Sheriff car. He got out and told us about a conversation he had with his wife regarding our camping situation. She had suggested to him that we be their overnight guests in their garage. That sounded better for us and he gave us the address and started to drive away. Then we heard a high pitch screeching sound like a fan belt slipping. As we looked towards the car we saw that Krishna had laid down behind one of the wheels and the car had started to drive over her. We yelled at the Sheriff to stop and ran over to Krishna, picked her up and could tell that she was badly hurt. We didn't know how badly hurt, but she was yelping enough to scare us.

When we got to the Sheriff's house we called our friends in San Antonio and asked them to come and get us so that we could take Krishna to the veterinarian as there were no vets in Sabinal. They told us that they could only come the next morning so we spent the night in the Sheriff's garage and barely slept because we were worried about Krishna and every once in awhile she would yelp in pain.

The next morning our friends picked us up and we left our bikes and baggage at the Sheriff's house. We took Krishna to the veterinarian as soon as we arrived in San Antonio. The x-rays showed that she had a broken right front leg but that it was a clean break and that it would heal easily. The vet bandaged it and put an aluminum splint on the leg and Krishna was back to her exuberant self.

ONE MAN'S SEARCH FOR THE DIVINE

The next morning we woke up to four inches of snow. So we decided to stay until the weather got better and that is when events would trigger a radical change in our plans.

The day after the snowfall we, of course, were stoned again. It seemed that Krishna had found a pair of Elizabeth's less then clean underwear and was running around the house with them in her mouth. It amused me and I began to laugh and for some reason Elizabeth got furious with me for laughing at the situation. Her anger seemed so absurd that I couldn't make sense out of it until later when she declared that she couldn't go through with this trip because of my disrespect. She decided to go back to Minneapolis. I knew that her decision to go back home was the right one and not because of any other reason then that this was my solemn journey and not hers.

A few days later, about the 20th of February Elizabeth boarded a flight back to Minneapolis and I was driven back to Sabinal to resume my journey, alone with Krishna. I sent Elizabeth's bike and baggage back to San Antonio with my friends and headed for the road. I had such a sense of relief at being alone and having to take care of only myself and Krishna who was very low maintenance. That first night sleeping alone near the highway and feeling so lonely, I cried myself to sleep and discovered a familiar inner strength that I had not felt since my decision to leave my wife.

The next morning after feeding Krishna her ration of dog food and having a breakfast of carrots and peanut butter we took off again on highway 90. Although my butt was getting sore again it seemed more tolerable than before and my legs seemed stronger. We did about sixty miles that day and we were on our way I kept thinking. About four o'clock that afternoon the rain/snow started again and I peddled to the next town, Bracketville, with the intention of calling the local Catholic Church and asking if there was a family that the priest could call to give me shelter since my funds were now almost depleted after paying for Krishna's accident and Elizabeth's plane ticket. I had told him about being a schoolteacher and writing a book, but he made up a story about how somebody had been charitable before and had been taken advantage of and people now were a lot more careful. I decided then to stay in the cheapest motel even though I only had about thirty dollars left of the money from the sale of my car. The motel was $8.00 and I got a six-pack of beer, some chips and dip and pigged out and fell asleep watching television.

The weather was clear the next morning and after replenishing my supplies of dog food, carrots, peanut butter and Payday candy bars I got back on highway 90 and decided to go and camp out by Amistad Recreational Area. This area is a man made lake/reservoir and it seemed like a place where I could get my bearings and

36

do some contemplation. It was also a good time of the year because the recreational season was closed and I would probably be alone.

I left highway 90 and went south a few miles on State Highway Spur 379 then took a dirt road that led to the shore. As I was riding down the dirt road, I noticed a deer running across the road about twenty feet in front of me and jumped over a low fence and disappeared into the thicket. There are feelings that we have that a part of the mind tries to put into words and as soon as it does the feelings seem to disappear. This time I think I had been alone long enough that my mind had quieted sufficiently so that I could savor this feeling of nature showing me her stuff. I had a sense that there was more to come.

I found a comfortable camping site about fifty yards from the shore. I gathered dead grass and made a cushion of sorts under my tent and rolled out the sleeping bag, gathered driftwood for a fire and felt like a teenager discovering aspects of myself that up until now were unknown. I lit a fire, fed Krishna and feasted on a carrot and peanut butter and finished off with a Payday candy bar. In France dinner with friends can last up to four hours because of the camaraderie and the wine and conversation and the leisurely way that the French dine. My friends that night were Krishna, the fire and firewood along with the cinders that rose up from the fire and made hissing and crakling sounds was like a conversation without words. I discovered that if I gaze at the rising cinders of a fire in a particular way, you see the whole tail of the cinders. Watching the cinders was a way that I caught up with the Now. I must have stared into the campfire for three or four hours. Anxiety was leaving my body and a deep sense of calm and peace took over. I could now go to sleep on my grass made mattress.

The following day I spent walking around the perimeter gathering firewood. I read Be here Now again for the third time. Reading this book constantly triggered a sense of hope for me that there was a possibility of something better in my future: a possibility of some kind of magic from the cosmos. I didn't know how it was going to happen, but I had a sense that it would. Everything that was going on in my life on this journey was new. I answered to no one and had no sense of obligation except to my dog's welfare. There was a constant sense of observing myself: my actions, my feelings, my thoughts. Although I was alone I wasn't lonely. I wondered how Michelle, my daughter was doing without me. She had seemed so mature when I had announced my leaving the family. She had told me that she knew that I would leave someday, she just didn't know when. The rest of the day was spent gazing into the campfire, feeding myself and Krishna and trying to make senseout of my life.

ONE MAN'S SEARCH FOR THE DIVINE

That night some clouds started to move in and after some time a light mist began to descend. Krishna and I climbed into the sleeping bag and I drifted off to sleep listening to the gentle pitter-patter of the rain on my pup tent. It must have been about two or three in the morning, (since I wasn't carrying a time piece I never knew exactly what time it was) when I awoke to water slowly creeping into my tent at the foot of my sleeping bag. The rain was now a full-blown storm and I went into a slight shock. "Now what do I do," I told myself. After taking some time to survey my situation with my flashlight, it was obvious from the intensity of the storm and the water rising at an alarming rate that to stay where I was, was not an option but what to do.

I decided to leave taking only my backpack. I put on my poncho, strapped my backpack on, put Krishna in the basket and took off back to the main road. When I got to the main road I felt lost and probably a bit traumatized and had no idea what to do next or which way to go and I remember thinking "this is crazy, I don't have any place to go, so I went back to my "home" by the lake. When I got back to my tent and looked inside with my flashlight, the sleeping bag was floating inside the tent. Again I thought, "leaving was crazy but this is even crazier" so I took off my backpack and threw it in the tent and left again. When I got to the main road, I decided to keep going West instead of going back towards San Antonio.

So here I was peddling down this dark road in the middle of the night with rain pouring down and feeling very sorry for myself with my dog, Krishna, in a basket in the front of the handlebars. Every now and then we would ride by a street light and I could see Krishna getting soaked by the rain. One time as we went by a light I happened to see her face squinting as the rain was hitting it and I was impressed by the lack of complaint on her part because up until then I was in a state of panic and feeling very sorry for myself. Seeing what I perceived was my dog's acceptance of this situation was just inspiring enough to give me the strength to keep on peddling. We probably did about twelve miles before we came upon the first motel.

Now I wasn't about to make a big fuss at that time of night, especially since I had a beard now and longer hair, so I knocked on the office door a couple of times and when no one answered I got back on my bike and kept going. I guess we went another four or five miles and arrived at another motel and again very timidly knocked on the office door with no answer. By now I also have accepted my dilemma and just kept peddling going West. A few miles further we found another motel and this one had a buzzer. I had already rehearsed in my mind what I was going to say to the owner: that I needed a room and in the morning I would have a friend wire me some money to pay for the room because I didn't think it was very safe to carry a lot of money with me. Within about a minute after I rang the buzzer a woman came to the door, looked at me through the window and held up her index finger as if to say one minute and she left. She soon came back with a key and opened the door, directed me to the room at the end of the motel and said: "I'll see you in the morning." Damn, I didn't even have a chance to tell her my story.

Krishna and I went to our room and I tell you I felt like a king. A warm room. A comfortable bed. A shower and a place to dry my wet clothes. Some simple pleasures can only be appreciated in a particular context. I was so grateful to be out of the rain and cold. Although I enjoyed the freedom and independence of being on the road, the creature comforts that this Motel provided seemed a lot more attractive. After showering, I went into a deep sleep and awoke refreshed and grateful wondering how I was going to deal with my day.

It was still raining when I walked out of my room towards the motel office. Once inside I went to the desk. The woman who had given me the key the night before was on the telephone and appeared upset. When she hung up she came to the counter and started to tell me that she had just received a call from one of her maids who told her that she wasn't coming in to work that day. Her maid had told her that there were about three inches of snow on the ground where she lived and was too freaked out to drive to the motel. What was even more upsetting is that the other maid had called in sick. As she was telling me her problems, I was thinking: "I know how to make beds, I know how to clean rooms and toilets." So when she finished telling me her problems, I said: "I know how to clean rooms and change and make beds. I'll be glad to help you out today and tomorrow if you need." "You're hired," she said and gave me cleaning supplies and a list of rooms that had to be made ready for new arrivals.

While I was in the middle of cleaning the first room, the manager, whom I later was told was also the owner, came to me and asked if I had had breakfast yet. I said no I had not and she said: "Well, you have to have breakfast. Follow me to the kitchen and I'll have the cook fix you some huevos rancheros." Whatever that was I didn't know but I was hungry enough to try anything. I went to the kitchen and was invited to sit down at the table and a plate of huevos rancheros was put in front of me along with a cup of coffee. I couldn't believe my eyes. Here was a plate with two eggs over easy with rice and refried beans with a couple of flour tortillas. My first huevos rancheros. I knew that this was an event that I would never forget and to this day when I have huevos rancheros I remember that memorable day in a small motel near the Mexican border and feeling the grace of the universe taking care of me.

I finished the list of rooms I had been given and called Elizabeth in Minneapolis and asked her to wire me some money. I made arrangements to go to my campsite

ONE MAN'S SEARCH FOR THE DIVINE

to pick up my backpack, sleeping bag and my tent. Then I spent the rest of the day washing and drying my stuff in the motel laundry. The owner, I'll call her Marie, told me that she was going through a divorce and had been stuck with taking care of this motel for quite a few months without a break. She asked me if I could watch the desk that night so she could go dancing with her boyfriend across the border. She said: "You can use the phone to call your daughter in Denver or your girlfriend in Minneapolis if you want. Whatever you need is available to you." So that night with a few instructions from Marie, I was now a motel manager and again felt so taken care of. I did call my daughter and Elizabeth. But mostly I just tried to take in my good fortune. The mind has a way of making it difficult to integrate the present. It was difficult at times to feel the moment because what was going on with me and my situation and the way that it was playing itself out was so unpredictable. Surrealistic comes to mind.

The following day it was still raining and I made arrangements with one of the guests to drive me to the local Western Union office to pick up the money Elizabeth had wired me and I spent another day in "paradise" cleaning rooms, eating huevos rancheros for breakfast and tacos for lunch and enchiladas for dinner. Without going to Mexico I was getting a taste of Mexican cuisine at its finest with much appreciation. That night I spent watching television in my room. Oh yes and what about Krishna? Well she just followed me around wherever I went with her right front leg in an aluminum splint. Leaving her in the room by herself was really not an option and besides she was my ambassador. People connected with me through her. That seems to happen with adults when either babies or pets are around.

When I awoke on the third morning at the motel, it was sunny out. I went to the desk and Marie told me that her maids were in and I told her that I was going to hit the road after my huevos rancheros. When I got packed and was ready to leave, I went to the desk to settle my bill and Marie said: "Are you crazy? You're the best thing that's come along in months. I'm not charging you a dime for the room or the meals. Then she gave me a care package of treats for me and one for Krishna. We hugged, I put Krishna in the basket in front of my bike and we hit the road with my pup tent on my bicycle rack with my dry sleeping bag on top and my dry backpack on my back. We were heading West again on highway 90. I felt exhilarated, refreshed, energetic and adventurous again.

I pedaled about thirty miles and took a short break in Comstock. I bought some bread, dog food, carrots, peanut butter and of course some Payday candy bars. After refreshments, we continued for another thirty miles and crossed the Pecos River Bridge. When I saw the view to my left just South of the bridge where the Pecos river dumps into the Rio Grande I knew that this is where I would camp out for the night. About a mile or two past the bridge I turned left onto a dirt road towards the bluff I had seen from the bridge. The road started to go down hill and the sand was loose so my bike started to slide and I lost control. Then it hit a rut, flipped over and I went flying over my bike and landed backwards on top of my backpack. I guess Krishna got thrown out of the basket because she landed on my lap, a bit freaked out. I was worried that she might have broken something or busted her splint, but she was just shaken up and curled up into my arms whimpering. I couldn't believe my luck at having fallen in such an intense way and not broken anything. I took a deep breath, took some time to take in what had happened and got back on my bike and continued on toward the bluff. When we got to the part where the two rivers meet, the bluff comes to a point and it is probably the most beautiful sight I had experienced so far. Again it was hard for me to take it all in.

This adventure was all new for me. Here I was a thirty-two year old man with an exwife and a ten-year-old daughter. I don't have a job. I don't have a place that I can call home. I had been working since I was fourteen years old. And since my daughter's birth I had been working two jobs to make ends meet. And now I've taken my life back and I have difficulty feeling the appreciation of this beautiful phenomenon in front of me. This was real. The Pecos River flowing into the Grand Canyon before my very eyes was real. Not a movie, not a picture but nature at her best and I was numb. The only experience I was having was my mind trying to figure things out and analyze the view. After about an hour of viewing the bluff and the two rivers meeting and the sound of waters rushing andthe blue sky and the fresh air and my dog and myself, my mind started to quiet down enough so that enthusiasm and gratitude and appreciation could be felt. Then I started to look for a campsite.

I finally located a spot close to the rivers so that the sound of the rushing water would cancel out the traffic noise from route 90. Again I built a fire, fed Krishna, dined on carrots and peanut butter and finished off my feast with dessert, a Payday candy bar. While lying in my sleeping bag, a familiar fear started to creep in. Here I was on this beautiful site with the light of the stars increasing with every minute, the faint sound of the rivers and just enough of a breeze so that I can tell that the air is moving across my sleeping bag and I start to get paranoid. What if some redneck finds me and kills me because I have long hair, I thought. Or what if some evil guy comes by and robs and kills me. Or what if some cowboys know where I am and come and kidnap me and tar and feather me. Now I can't even enjoy where I am anymore. I'm not afraid that some wolfmight come looking for my dog Krishna and try to eat it or that some bear may come and maul me or even that a rattlesnake (I've been told to be aware of them) might crawl into my sleeping bag and bite me. No. I'm afraid of human beings. How crazy and paranoid is that? What kind of messages am I walking around with about human beings?

ONE MAN'S SEARCH FOR THE DIVINE

I was never hurt by or afraid of nature. When I was six years old and lived in Lac Megantic, Quebec in Canada I used to play in the woods by myself in the summertime. Our house was the last one on the gravel street. I always felt safe in the forest. I often would lie down on the leaf covered forest floor and look straight up at the sky and watch the clouds magically drift by like huge spaceships or watch the tops of the trees swaying back and forth to the movement of the wind and listen to the rustling leaves. Sometimes there would be a hawk that would just hover in the sky above me. As a six year old I was never afraid that an animal or a human being would come along and hurt me. Many times I saw wildlife and I think they saw me but I never felt the need to talk to them or touch them. It was enough just to see them and observe their behavior and feel their wildness. Sometimes I would take a nap and wake up wondering where I was or what time it was. Not that knowing the time was important but often times in the summer I would miss dinner because the sun set so late. I would often freak out my mother because she had no idea where I was and sometimes I would show up for dinner after the dining room table had been cleared and the food had been put away. My punishment for being a "bad boy" was to go to bed without eating. That never bothered me because I always had a stash of crackers and peanut butter somewhere around my bed.

Across the road from our house in Lac Megantic there was a field of hay. That was another favorite play area in the summertime. After the hay was cut and put into piles, the kids would run around the field and play hide and seek. We would hide in the haystacks. There would be all these interesting little bugs in the hay. It didn't bother me then that they crawled over me. They didn't bite me and besides they tickled. Did I mention the smell of the freshly cut hay? Freshly cut hay has a fragrance that is more aromatic than any perfume my mother ever wore. It is an aroma that stimulates certain brain cells to release endorphins that are akin to euphoria. Whenever I smell it today as an adult, I'm reminded of those days in the hay fields in Lac Megantic. I was in this sleeping bag on this beautiful bluff where the Pecos River meets the Rio Grande and there is Mexico just a stone's throw away and I can't even enjoy it because I'm afraid that some human being is going to come along and hurt me. How did I get to this insane place? When did I start to feel so unsafe in this world? Not only unsafe but also paranoid. It never occurred to me to link my paranoia with the trauma that I had experienced as a seven-year old. I finally fell asleep after asking Krishna to alert me if anything suspicious approached.

The following morning it was time to leave my beautiful but scary space. We hit route 90 again going West and moved at a pretty good pace now. The numbness in my butt was gone as I had become used to the seat. My legs had become quite strong. When I had a tail wind my backpack would act as a sail and I just rode along effortlessly grateful that it wasn't raining. What a relief. I must mention an observation

42

I had as I rode close to the shoulder of the road. There was usually a ditch between the shoulder and the open fields.

It was like the locals, whoever they were, used the ditch as their personal dump. I saw beer cans, beer bottles, soft drink cans, mostly Dr. Pepper, and trash of all kinds. The ditch was like a continuous trash can. Another thing that I observed was that it seemed that the whole state was fenced in. Everywhere I looked there were fences between the ditches and the fields. If I had wanted to camp out away from the road to be safe I would have to jump the fence and ignore the "no trespassing" signs.

After about three hours of peddling, I took a break off the road under one of the few oak trees I had seen. As I sat drinking some water and eating some two-day-old dried bread and letting Krishna stretch her legs and do her bodily functions I notice about a half dozen Mexicans hiding in a culvert and trying not to be noticed. I figured that they were either waiting for a ride or waiting for dark to continue on their journey. I guessed that they probably were thirsty and a bit hungry so I gave them the bottle of water I had and the rest of the bread. Soon after, I got back on my bike because I didn't want to bring attention to them. About two o'clock that afternoon the clouds started to accumulate and t started getting colder. Now the fun was starting to disappear again because it looked like it was going to rain. About four PM it started to sprinkle so I put on my poncho, covered Krishna with a towel and wished for the rain to stop, but the rain just intensified and I was starting to get bummed and depressed and a bit panicky. "Not again," I told myself. The further down the road I went the more desperate I got. As I was peddling and feeling sorry for myself, I heard what sounded like my own voice in my head saying:

"What are you doing? Where are you going?" "Well, I'm going to the Lama Foundation." "Yes but why are you doing it this way? What you are doing is not very practical. You are the one who decided to do it this way. You are the only one who can change the way you do it." And as I heard that, I thought: "That's true I am the only one who can change the way I do this."

The realization that this adventure was in my hands now gave me such a sense of relief that the depression lifted immediately and my strength came back and even though it was now raining with more intensity I was not bummed. I realized that I wasn't bound by early decisions but what to do. I started to plan in my head to ditch my bike at the next town and hitch hike. Even hitch hiking was better than this. At the pace that I was going, it would be Summer before I got to the Lama foundation. I saw very clear instructions in my head. It's hard to explain. It wasn't a voice that I heard. It was like a Polaroid picture.

ONE MAN'S SEARCH FOR THE DIVINE

I planned to go to the bus depot at the next town and ship my bike and my pup tent and any extra baggage back to San Antonio. With a newly found sense of enthusiasm, I peddled to the next town as fast as my legs could take me.

The next town was Sanderson. It was dark when I biked up to the diner at the Eastern end of town. The rain was now coming down in sheets, but my spirits were up. I entered the diner with Krishna by my feet and asked the manager where the bus depot was.

"This is it," he said.

"I have to ship something to San Antonio," I said.

"You'll have to take care of that with the bus driver and by the way he's about an hour late. He should be arriving in about twenty minutes."

So far so good, I thought. And all of the constriction that I felt biking in this cold rain and the depression I had been feeling was lifting like a fever from my body. I was starting to get pretty liberated about the decision I had made. I thanked the manager, went outside and got my bike ready for shipping. I took the bike tools out of my backpack and put anything that was unnecessary in the box that contained the pup tent and got it ready for shipping as soon as the bus arrived.

A few minutes later the Greyhound bus arrived and I talked to the driver about shipping my bike and the box holding the tent and the incidentals to San Antonio. He said that I would have to ship it collect because he had no way of determining the weight of the bike or the box. I filled out the shipping form and put Dianne, my sister's name, on the waybill. And as the bus drove away with my stuff, I felt so freed up. I was also relieved because I only had a few dollars left. At the same time that the bus was pulling out, the border patrol guy I had seen in the restaurant walked out and as he was going towards his station wagon I asked him where the cheapest motel was. "It's at the Western end of town," he said. I thanked him and started walking in the direction he indicated.

After a few steps he said, "Hop in. I'll give you a ride." Again I'm feeling really good about my decision to hitch hike and also more and more starting to feel something inside of me opening up not to anything specific but just an opening up of energy that felt a little bit like when I would get stoned. Some of these feelings are hard to describe.

I got dropped off at this cheap motel and went inside to register. The fee was six dollars. I signed in, got the key and went to the room. When we walked in there

44

was a thin layer of dampness on the floor. The room was barely larger than the bed with a pipe stove in the corner and a bathroom with a shower and I felt like I was in a chateau compared to what I had been experiencing. I fed Krishna and heated up a can of FrancoAmerican spaghetti and meatballs on the stove that I had saved for a special occasion and feasted with much delight. The only thing missing was perhaps a glass of Chianti wine.

After dinner a hot shower and a bed. I spread some of my wet clothes around the stovepipe, I wrote a note to Dianne with the copy of the waybill for my stuff and went to sleep. Life is good.

The following morning it was still raining when I went to the desk to check out and mail the envelope to my sister. The manager and a couple of other men were standing around talking when I walked in. After turning in my key, I asked what it was like hitchhiking in Sanderson.

"Not all that great," said one of the men.

"Especially when it's raining," said the manager.

"Where can I get a righteous breakfast," I asked?

"Well, there's a diner at the East end of town that will feed you to your satisfaction," said the man with the engineer cap.

The rain had turned into a light mist by now. Krishna and I walked to the diner, which is also the bus depot, and I hoped that the prices would also be righteous because my funds were depleting fast. When we walked into the diner it was bustling with morning breakfast activity and we got a table by the doorway. To my relief I could get a huevos rancheros and coffee for less than four dollars. As I ate my breakfast, the thought of spending my time in nature seemed great when the weather is mild and I could enjoy a acampfire and eat my carrots and peanut butter but when it's raining and cold, shelter and creature comforts are for me. Roughing it had its limits. I finished every morsel on my plate, paid my bill and returned to the West end of town to start my hitchhiking experience. The walk to the West end was exhilarating.

"I'm on my way,

" I kept thinking over and over like a mantra. Once we were at the West end, I put my backpack under an overhang by a store, and with a grin from ear to ear, I held Krishna under my poncho with my left arm while I kept my thumb up with my right. About an hour later I was still on the same spot when the fine mist turned into a light rain. Many Recreational Vehicles of all sizes drove by. The fact that these RV's didn't invite

45

ONE MAN'S SEARCH FOR THE DIVINE

me to ride with them was slightly disappointing, but it didn't erase the ear-to-ear grin that I had because "I WAS ON MY WAY."

There was a clearing across the street from where I was standing with a view of the railroad tracks and the hills beyond. About every hour or so a locomotive pulling a long line of freight cars going East would stop, drop off freight cars and add others then pullout. Sometimes the train would just keep going without stopping. Seeing this reminded me of my friend, Speedy, who was a free spirit and pretty much, lived on the road. He also had a dog. A few weeks before I left Minneapolis with Elizabeth, Speedy dropped by my apartment for a visit and to share about his recent train ride from Seattle.

Speedy told me that he had hitchhiked to Washington state to visit some friends and his friends suggested that he could return to Minneapolis via the rail lines. He told me that he was walking East along the tracks with his dog when a freight train stopped and the engineer invited him to ride on the locomotive with him. He said that he and the engineer smoked a joint on the ride and that he thought it was a great way to travel. Speedy, Elizabeth and I had dinner together and then I started talking about a book I had been reading that was a true inspiration for me. He said, "I know which book you're talking about. It's Be Here Now by Ram Dass." "I can't believe that you're reading this also," I said. That night Speedy stayed with us and left the following morning and I haven't heard from him since. That short visit with Speedy I was realizing as I was standing there in the rain hitchhiking with my dog under my poncho was all a part of this cosmic play that seemed to be unfolding for me and the thought of riding the train started to become a possibility.

It was now about two thirty in the afternoon and not even a hint of someone wanting to give me a ride. There were still low lying clouds and the fog was rolling in, but the rain had stopped. Route 90 is a main highway going west toward El Paso. Semi trucks and trucks of all sizes drove by. It seemed that every other vehicle was an RV and they were of all sizes and opulence but no ride. And the more I noticed the trains going East the more I opened up to the possibility of doing a "Speedy." About that time one of the menwhom I had talked to in the motel lobby that morning, the one with the engineer hat, pulled up in his station wagon, rolled down his window and asked where I was going.

"I'm going to New Mexico by way of El Paso," I said. "Well, there'll be a train coming through here in about forty-five minutes going to El Paso. You might think of hopping on it." Can this possibly be happening, I'm thinking. But I'm still a little bit paranoid so I said, "Are you hopping on it too?" "No, I'm not. I'm the engineer who'll be taking it to El Paso. There'll be a boxcar open near the engine and there'll be a boxcar open near the middle and there'll be a boxcar open near the end. The

46

middle one will stop just about over there," as he pointed to the direction just across the street from where I was standing. "You can go get yourself ready to hop on over there. Wait for the train to stop. Throw your stuff on board then climb up. Situate yourself in one of the corners where it is the safest to ride. Don't do anything stupid and don't get off until the train has arrived in the yards and come to a complete stop in El Paso." I thanked him and I grabbed my backpack and walked towards the area that the engineer had pointed to.

There was a part of me that had difficulty accepting my good fortune. It seemed as though I was in an altered state. Could this really be happening to me? This is a good thing and it's happening to me. Hopping a freight train was something every kid dreams about and here I am thirty-two years old and the child in me is struggling to accept all this. While I was standing about twenty feet from the tracks, an official looking station wagon with the sign "Border Patrol" written on the side pulled up. The driver rolled down his window. I recognized him as the same guy that had given me a ride to my motel room the night before. "Planning on hopping the train," he asked with a smile? What was I going to do say "no." Besides this wasn't my idea. The engineer gave me his OK.

"Yes," I said, "the engineer suggested that it would be OK."

"That's a good way to travel," the border patrol guy said. "If you hadn't hopped the train we would have found you a ride with a trucker. We don't like hitchhikers to stay in town overnight. We like to avoid any possible trouble."

"Thanks. I appreciate your consideration."

While he waited there for the train to arrive we chatted a bit. I told him that I was a high school teacher on sabbatical and I was in the process of writing a book about my adventures. And he talked a bit about his work and how sympathetic he was to the Mexicans who try to cross over but that he had a job to do.

Then the train arrived. It moved very slowly. And sure enough there was an open boxcar near the front. When the train came to a full stop there was an open boxcar almost exactly where the engineer said it would be. As I approached to hop on, I was a little bit hesitant with the Border Patrol officer sitting there. I looked towards the engine and there was the engineer waving me on to the car. So I put my backpack on board then Krishna and then I pulled myself up on the boxcar and looked around. It was pretty dirty with black soot all over the floor. There was brown paper from the floor to about six feet up attached to the inside walls all the way around. About ten minutes after I got on board the train started to pull away. The border patrol guy waved at me and then drove away.

47

ONE MAN'S SEARCH FOR THE DIVINE

After we had cleared the town, I surveyed my situation and saw that some housekeeping needed to happen. So I pulled off some of the brown paper from the sides of the boxcar and covered a space about eight by ten feet in the corner. Then I sat at the doorway and watched the scenery go by. We were moving pretty slow, perhaps twenty to twenty five miles an hour.

When we arrived in Marathon about an hour later, the train stopped and the engine moved freight cars around, dropped some off and attached others and my paranoia kicked in again. "Oh, Oh," I thought to myself, "they know exactly what car I'm in and they're going to come and get me and tar and feather me." And no sooner was I thinking that, then my string of freight cars were reattached to the rest of the train and we were off again. It still took me awhile to feel safe and comfortable. I went back to the doorway and sat down with my legs dangling over the side and talked myself into enjoying the scenery and my good fortune. Finally, the light mist that had been there all afternoon turned to a light drizzle then snow. Watching the scenery go by as the snow was coming down was divine and I felt grateful for the first time since I left San Antonio. After about an hour of forced enjoyment, I went back to the corner of the freight car and had a little snack of carrots and peanut butter. After feeding Krishna it was now dark so I unrolled the sleeping bag across the carpet of brown paper and after Krishna crawled in (that bitch always seemed to get in before me) I got in.

After about twenty minutes, I felt a warm fluid on my thighs and realized that Krishna had just taken a leak on my leg. I got angry and yelled at her and she scurried out of the sleeping bag. She looked so pathetic standing there in the dark and shivering with her right front leg in that aluminum splint that my anger passed quite rapidly and invited her to crawl back in with me. Besides she was keeping me warm aside from her peeing on my leg.

We had been lying there maybe about another hour when the freight car started to rock back and forth. It seemed that every once in a while the car would hit a piece of track and start to rock back and forth. Sometimes this rocking would last for fifteen, twenty minutes and I would brace my body and eventually get very stiff. Actually it was kind of foolish for me to try to brace myself because the whole car was rocking and bracing myself did not change anything. And as I realized this, that same little voice I had heard a few times earlier on my trip said: "Why don't you just relax. You're not going to be thrown back and forth across the car." So instead of trying to resist the rocking by tightening up I relaxed and let the car rock me. It was one of the best massages I had everhad and I finally fell asleep.

48

As we arrived closer to El Paso, the train started to slow down. I woke up about then and watched the town go by through the open door. It was about four thirty or five in the morning. I rolled up my sleeping bag which smelled like dog pee as did my jeans. We eventually pulled into the train yard with its multiple tracks. I remembered what the engineer had said: "Don't do anything stupid like trying to get on or off while the cars are moving." My boxcar stopped just a few yards from another engine and as I got off with my stuff and walked away I heard someone say: "Where are you off to?" I looked around and heard again from the engineer on the locomotive on the next track: "Where are you off to?" "Oh hi," I said, " I'm going to Albuquerque."

"Too bad you're not going to Tucson, we're leaving in about twenty minutes."

I had to process this invitation real quick. Maybe the "Universe" wants me to go to Tucson, I thought. Then again what am I going to do once I'm there? I decided that Albuquerque was the direction that was for me. I began walking towards the large illuminated Greyhound sign I had seen earlier. Taking the bus was not an option for me as I didn't have the money for a ticket, but I did want to clean up and get re-oriented and then make my next move.

Once I got to the depot, I checked my stuff into a locker. While I was busy storing my stuff, Krishna was making friends with a guy with long hair. Krishna was always such a hit with her front leg in that aluminum splint. As I approached her, the hippie, (I'll call him Mike) looked up at me and gave me a smile and asked: "Your dog?"

"Yes," I said.

"Her name is Krishna and she's quite a charmer. We just hitched a ride by train and we're headed for Albuquerque."

"I'm heading for Albuquerque too. That's where I live. As a matter of fact, my room-mate is coming to pick me up and you and Krishna can ride along with us. I just got in from Buenos Aires. I've been away for six weeks." I excused myself and went to the men's room and cleaned up a bit and tried to get the pee smell off my jeans. I got myself a cup of coffee, gave Krishna some water and rejoined Mike.

After waiting for about an hour, Mike got a page and when he got back to me he said that his buddy's car had blown up on his way to El Paso and he would have to find another way home. So Mike said: "Why don't we try to hop a train?" "Let's do it," I said and we picked up our stuff and headed for the train yard.

ONE MAN'S SEARCH FOR THE DIVINE

We walked over to where the locomotives were standing to try and find a train leaving for Albuquerque. After about a half hour of looking for someone, I started to feel a bit paranoid again. "What if some redneck sees these two hippies with a dog and backpacks and alerts the police and we're arrested?" Then we saw an engineer and asked him where and when the next train was leaving for Albuquerque.

"Not on this line." He Said. "You have to go to the other line for Albuquerque."

"Where can I find that other line?"

"You see those other engines that say Union Pacific?"

"Yeah."

"That's it."

Mike and I picked up our gear and walked over to the Union Pacific line. On the way there we met some of the workers in the yard and asked them when the next train to Albuquerque was leaving. "There was one that left about twenty minutes ago," one of them said. Then they started checking out some of the other trains heading North that we could possibly take to catch up to the one that had just left. The only thing that worked was a freight train leaving in about three hours and we could hop on that one. Mike and I decided to hitchhike instead and if we didn't get a ride within a couple of hours we would come back to the rail line and try again. As we walked towards route I 25 Mike said: "I can't believe how friendly these railroad guys are." "I know," I said, "I've been told by just about everybody how dangerous it is to hop freight trains because hobos are territorial and can beat you up if you try to hone in on their territory or the railroad people will turn you in to the police and instead what I experience is how helpful and friendly they are. Also, I was warned about how dangerous it is for a hippie to hitchhike in Texas because the cowboys, and rednecks are looking for guys with long hair so that they can tar and feather them. I've had nothing but good luck from everyone from the Sheriff in some of the towns to the Border Patrol, to the railroad people. It's not like they know upon seeing me at first that I'm a traveling schoolteacher on sabbatical and writing a book about my adventures. "

"Maybe the Universe is just working through these people and paving the way for you," Mike said.

"I don't know, but I'm starting to feel pretty well taken care of."

"When you open up to receiving, it just flows. Grace does not force itself on anyone," Mike said.

Andre Patenaude

I had already started to feel some benevolent power or force or something taking care of me based on my experiences so far. It's not that I planned any of the details in advance. My plan was to go to the Lama Foundation to see if they could help me figure out what to do with my life. Biking to get there was too slow and not much fun when it was cold and raining. The camping was an adventure but distracting me from my purpose of getting to the Foundation. So it seemed to me that some power was assisting me in my purpose. Maybe the bad weather was all a part of it. I kept a lot of these kinds of thoughts to myself because they seemed a little too radical and woo woo to share with others.

Now I have a traveling companion who seems to have been sent to assist me. Mike's demeanor was always pleasant and optimistic. I never told him, but I made up a story about him as we went along that he was an angel sent by those Spirits that Mary in Ames, Iowa had sent to watch over me. And for that matter my dog Krishna had been sent to me to act as an ambassador, which in many ways she was. Without her, I probably would not have connected with Mike or been seen as safe and un-threatening. I looked back and saw that Krishna had to suffer a broken leg for me to listen and follow what I knew was the right thing to do and that was to travel without Elizabeth because I made her such a distraction, a beautiful distraction at that but a distraction nevertheless.

I'm with this other "guardian angel" in the flesh and we're going to go and hitch-hike together on route I 25 to Albuquerque, two long haired hippies, two backpacks and a dog standing on the side of the road with our thumbs out. The chances of get-ting a ride seemed pretty remote to me, but we tried it anyway and we always had the option of hopping a freight train if we didn't get a ride. Within fifteen minutes, a guy in his mid twenties driving a Volkswagen bug stopped to ask us where we were going. "We're going to Albuquerque," Mike said.

"You'll be here all day if I don't pick you up," the driver said.

"I'll take you across the state line into New Mexico. You'll have better luck there." So we crammed into his VW. I sat in the back with Krishna and the two backpacks.

The driver had just been driving around and smoking a joint. He was a Marine and had been in Viet Nam for a year and had been discharged about three months prior. He wasn't working and had trouble relating to his life outside the military. He brought back enough weed to keep him and his friends high for months, he told us. Looking for a job was just not a priority. Finally, we were across the state line and about ten miles into New Mexico when the driver pulled over to the shoulder and let us out. He handed each of us a joint that he said came from Nam. We thanked him,

51

ONE MAN'S SEARCH FOR THE DIVINE

said good bye and then he drove across the two lanes and the middle grass strip and drove back to Texas.

Mike and I immediately lit up one joint and shared it. Within minutes, we were both pretty high and it seemed that New Mexico did have a different energy, it felt so much freer and expansive. And again here we are two longhaired looking hippies with backpacks and a dog hitchhiking and totally stoned. We both felt that we were on top of the world and within twenty minutes a guy driving a white pickup stopped and asked us where we were going. When we said: "Albuquerque." He said: "That's where I'm going. Hop on."

We put our stuff in the back of the pick up and we got into the cab with me holding Krishna on my lap and we were on our way. Again I started to feel so taken care of. I kept thinking that maybe there is something to this Universe business and maybe the "spirits" were guiding me. Because when you think about it: here's two scruffy looking guys hitchhiking with backpacks and a dog and we got rides which went way beyond my expectations especially when people often told me how dangerous it was to hitchhike and "wasn't I afraid that some serial killer might pick me up and torture and kill me." When we told him about the last ride and that we were smoking weed from Viet Nam, he perked up and said that he also had recently returned from "Nam" and had not smoked the "fine Nam weed" since being discharged. And of course we shared our other joint with the driver.

The rest of the ride seemed like a blur and when we arrived in Albuquerque he took us right to Mike's doorstep. Mike invited me to stay the rest of the week with him and his biker buddies. "You can crash on the living room floor," he said "and make yourself at home. This coming Sunday we'll ride down to Santa Fe with my friends and you can continue on to the Lama Foundation from there. Again I felt taken care of and again with people who didn't judge me or criticize me for the way that I looked or for my lack of funds.

Each day I was invited to share in the meals and since Mike also had a dog, Krishna had a good supply of dog food. Every night Mike's friends would show up on their Harley choppers. They didn't fit the stereotypical biker that again I had many ideas about.

They didn't appear to be criminal types. I never saw guns or knives or three hundred pound tattooed bikers. Just a bunch of guys who worked during the day, drank beer, smoked weed and partied at night with their girlfriends. I had been accepted by them as an equal and also felt a familiar camaraderie that I had not felt since I was a student at Augsburg College. During the week, I got a chance to wash my sleeping bag and my clothes and also to take a couple of warm showers. Sunday morning arrived and after breakfast I was told by Mike to get my stuff ready to ride. I was to ride behind him and hold Krishna in my arms with my backpack on my back. About eleven AM we headed East of town towards Old Highway 66 and met up with fifteen other bikers all riding choppers, some had girl friends others were solo. After going eastbound about eighteen miles, we turned north at Tijeras, NM on highway 14, and the Turquoise Trail. What I realized was that bikers aren't that much of in a hurry to get somewhere, especially as a group. They prefer the scenic route and the scenic route we were taking. After passing through Cedar Crest, a little town North of Tijeras, we were now in the high desert. I was on Mike's bike with Krishna in my arms behind ten other bikers. She seemed to be enjoying the ride with the air blowing in her face and her ears flowing back and her tongue hanging to the side similar to how we see dogs hanging their heads out of car windows. As for me I had finally quieted my mind enough to start enjoying what was going on as it was happening. "Being in the now," is Ram Dass' theme in his book Be Here Now, which had become my Bible and the only book I was carrying. By now it was "dog eared" and stained but my constant companion. I had finally relaxed into the ride and I was ecstatic.

Eventually, we got to Madrid, NM about thirty miles from Tijeras and the road became curvy and hilly. I can see why bikers have such a love affair with their bikes. Riding through the mountains on curvy and hilly roads that present a new scene around every curve was absolutely exhilarating riding behind the driver, it must be even more so in the front, sitting on 1300 ccs and in charge of your own destiny.

After another sixteen or so miles, we took Cerrito Road again another side road instead of taking the freeway. We arrived in Santa Fe about one o'clock and went looking for a Mexican restaurant on the Santa Fe Trail near Loretto's Chapel. There was quite a bit of activity and pedestrian traffic at this time and again I got to try some new Mexican cuisine. Mike knew that I didn't have any money and offered to treat me and suggested a chicken burrito. Another opportunity to develop my culinary intelligence. First it's huevos rancheros and now a chicken burrito. I found that quite satisfying and after lunch one of the bikers suggested that we go visit the Loretto Chapel. Loretto Chapel we were told held a modern miracle. It's no longer a place of worship but a museum mainly to display the "miracle" for tourists. The Miraculous Staircase is what is on display. Apparently the Sisters of Loretto had trekked all the way to Santa Fe from St. Louis, Missouri to start a school at the behest of Bishop Jean Batiste Lamy in1852. The bishop was seeking to spread the faith and bring an educational system to this new territory. To go along with the school and their Catholic faith, it was decided that they needed a chapel. So in 1873 land was purchased and the chapel built according to the Gothic Revival-style patterned after King Louis IX's Sainte-Chapelle in Paris in contrast to the adobe churches already in the area. The

ONE MAN'S SEARCH FOR THE DIVINE

Chapel was completed in 1878, but a staircase had not been built to the choir loft and the only way to the loft was by ladder. The sisters did not feel comfortable with the prospect of having to climb up and down the ladder every time that they wanted to sing during the celebration of the Mass. It was inconvenient and dangerous due to the long habits that they wore. Because building a traditional staircase would have taken up too much room in the sanctuary, the sisters prayed to the patron saint of carpenters, St. Joseph to intercede for them to create a way to get up to the choir loft. They prayed for nine straight days. On the day after their novena ended a shabby looking stranger appeared at their door. He told the nuns he would build them a staircase but that he needed total privacy and locked himself in the chapel for three months. He used a small number of primitive tools including a square, a saw and some warm water and constructed a spiral staircase entirely of non-native wood.

The identity of the carpenter is not known for as soon as the staircase was finally finished he was gone. Many witnesses, upon seeing the staircase, think it was built by St. Joseph himself, as a miraculous occurrence. The legend claims that the mystery had never been satisfactorily solved as to who the carpenter was or where he got his lumber, and that there were no reports of anyone seeing lumber delivered or even seeing the man come and go while the construction was being done. Since he disappeared before he was paid the Sisters of Loretto offered a reward for the identity of the man, but it was never claimed.

After the Chapel, I started to get anxious to get on the road again and Mike and his friends took me to the highway leading towards Taos and eventually the Lama Foundation. So they took me to the corner of the Taos Highway, U.S 84. As my friends were refueling at the gas station on the same corner, I crossed the street with my backpack and Krishna. Before my friends finished refueling, a VW bug driven by a young guy of about twenty-three stopped. He said that he was going close to Taos and that I could ride with him as far as he was going. I put my backpack in the back seat and Krishna and I sat in the passenger seat in the front. About twenty miles further we saw a man hitchhiking and the driver pulled up and picked him up also. Krishna and I moved to the back seat with my backpack and the other guy's backpack and the new rider rode in the front passenger seat.

At Española, New Mexico we changed from US route 84 to NM route 68. So far the conversation in the car was almost non-existent save "where are you going," and "where are you coming from." We also exchanged names. I'll call the driver Doug and the other hitchhiker John. I think we were all pretty road weary and men being men, conversation was not all that important.

54

About five miles short of Taos, Doug pulled over to the side of the road at the entrance to a dirt road and told us that he was dropping us off because he was leaving the hightway. John asked Doug to call his friend in San Cristobol to come and pick us up as he was expecting him. It was still daylight and John and I started walking with our backpacks on our backs and Krishna walking along side of us with her leg in the aluminum splint.

John was a man of about forty-five maybe fifty with salt and pepper hair, more salt then pepper. His beard was about the same and he had wrinkles under and around his eyes that gave him a perpetually sad look. He was physically fit and had large and calloused hands. As we walked I asked John where he was coming from. He replied: "Right now I'm just coming back from Seattle. I left here three weeks ago not knowing what direction I was going. I decided to be adventurous and go in the direction my first ride took me to. It took me North to Colorado and then West and finally after a couple of days and a half dozen rides I arrived in Seattle. I have some friends there so I connected with them and spent a few days with them and then headed back and of course took my time. I'm never in a hurry when I hitchhike. What about you, where are you coming from?" he asked.

"Well, I'm coming from San Antonio," I said. "I started out on a ten-speed bike about two weeks ago, ditched my bike because it was too slow and I got tired of the rain. Then I hopped a freight train to El Paso and hitchhiked with someone I met at the Greyhound bus depot and on to Albuquerque. Then got a ride with a bunch of bikers on choppers to Santa Fe. I'm on my way to the Lama Foundation. Have you heard of it?" "Oh yeah, I've been there many times. They do great meditation retreats there.

"Are you going there to meditate?" he asked.

"I'm just going to check it out and see what's going on. So John what brought you out here to New Mexico?"

"Six years ago, I walked into my business partner's office in San Francisco, we were in construction together, and threw my keys on his desk and told him that I was leaving. I was burned out and I wasn't very happy. I had a beautiful home in Marin County, my kids were grown up and my wife was more interested in her social life than in our relationship and I started to feel used and burned out."

"That makes a lot of sense," I said. "It just seems that we men are straddled with the role of not only being the bread winner, but also having to provide for a life style that we don't necessarily enjoy and that seems to be more and more demanding. And eventually we burn out. I saw my father and father-in-law both burn out and die at the age of fifty nine and I knew that I was next so I left my marriage. You know John, I read about a statistic regarding people who go out for a loaf of bread or a pack of cigarettes and don't come back. For every woman who goes out and doesn't come back there are two hundred men. That tells me something about the stress that we have put ourselves under."

"My wife and I saw a therapist," said John "and we split up amicably. Financially, she is set for the rest of her life. I took a little something with me and decided to settle out here after having visited a few times. I built myself an adobe hut, something I had always wanted to do. It's just one large round room with windows in all four directions. The windowsills are deep enough to take a nap in the afternoon if you want. I made closefriends with some neighbors and live a simple life as stress free as possible."

"Do you hitchhike often?" I asked.

"Once a year I hit the road just to get a feel for the country and the people. Last year I went east, but I never go East of the Mississippi."

We continued walking and John told me that he was wondering if Doug had ever made the call. Finally, it got dark and walking along side the road became a bit of a hazard at times, as there were no streetlights to illuminate our path. We ended up walking the rest of the way to Taos and once we found a phone booth, John called his friend. He was home and no he didn't get a call from Doug and that's probably because he had been out until just a few minutes ago and yes he's on his way to pick us up. John told him to look for us and a dog walking along side the road.

About a half hour later his friend, I'll call him Steve, arrived. It was obvious that John and Steve were close and had a lot of affection for each other. It was the first time I had seen John smile. We hopped into his SUV and within fifteen minutes we pulled into Steve's driveway.

Steve was a tall man of about forty with long black hair and a full black beard. He wore glasses and seemed to have a constant smile. He was very attentive and loving which for me created some unease. Nevertheless most of the attention went to John and I could just be an observer, which for me was the most comfortable.

Steve prepared a vegetarian meal for us with some beer by candlelight and brought us up on the latest events. The Moody Blues were playing in the background. Steve had their whole collection of albums. Then the attention turned to me. Steve looked at me with so much love that I started to get scared and he noticed it. "I see that you have been traumatized in your life and you are scared of love," Steve said. "I also see that you have a lot of courage and that you're looking for something to fulfill your life

Andre Patenaude

and I don't have any doubt that you will find it."

At the time, I felt ashamed and extremely uncomfortable. I could tell that Steve was not a homosexual and that he was safe to be with. But the feeling of paranoia was very intense. Steve ignored the situation and returned talking with John. After dinner, I asked Steve if he had any Maalox.

"What do you want Maalox for?" he asked.

"Because my ulcer is acting up and that always helps me."

"You have an ulcer?"

"Yes."

"How long have you had and ulcer?"

"Since my early twenties."

"Let me get something for you." Steve said.

Steve left the room and after a few minutes returned with a briefcase. He opened it and it was full of baggies containing all sorts of herbs. He took out three different baggies and put about a fourth of a teaspoon of each herb in a glass and filled it with water and said:

"Drink this down very quick."

I drank it down and almost gagged. It was some of the foulest stuff I ever drank. A few minutes later I was on the floor with a burning pain in my stomach then my stomach started cramping. Steve was on the floor next to me and coached me to take some deep breaths and within a few minutes the cramping abated and I could talk again.

"Wow, that was really intense," I said.

"Yes it was," said Steve. "And now how do you feel?"

"A bit better, but I still have some burning in my stomach."

"That's the cayenne burning in there. If there was any bleeding, it would cauterize it. The golden seal and myrrh in the mixture will destroy the bacteria causing your ulcer.

ONE MAN'S SEARCH FOR THE DIVINE

Steve made up a little baggie for me of golden seal, myrrh and cayenne pepper all mixed together and said: "take about a half teaspoon of this mixture in a full glass of water every day for the next ten days and your ulcer will disappear." And he was right.

"You can stay here tonight," Steve said, "and tomorrow I'll introduce you to the community in Arroyo Hondo, a little town just North of here."

The next morning, I was served some granola with soymilk for breakfast and then John drove me to Arroyo Hondo. This was a community of hippies: men, women, and kids. The people were of all ages, my age, younger and older. They were all welcoming of Krishna and me. She with her aluminum splint especially fascinated the kids. They took care of her as though she was a doll.

These people were in the middle of building an adobe add-on to an already existing hut. I volunteered to assist them for my board and that worked out for everybody. The next day, one of the men suggested that I check out a hot spring along the Western bank of the Rio Grand River just a few miles West of town. So I took Krishna with me and we walked through the village of Arroyo Hondo. This is a small-unincorporated town with unpaved streets and with mostly a Mexican population of about eight hundred people.

There was hardly anyone on the streets except for a couple of children and a few dogs. We followed the directions to the bridge over the Rio Grande and on the West side of the river there was a trail that zigzagged up the side of the bluff. Apparently this once was an old trail that the pioneers etched out as they continued West. I walked up the first leg of the "zig"going south and just as the trail turned to "zag" North, I could see a pool of water next to the river with steam rising from it. I took Krishna in my arms and carried her down the side of the bluff and to the pool. Again another sight which was difficult for me to integrate. Here was this pool of hot mineral water with a sandy bottom, only about ten feet from the river and surrounded by snow.

I tested the water and it was at a tolerable temperature, so I took my clothes off and got in. The pool was probably big enough for maybe three or four adults. It was about four feet deep with a sandy bottom.

As I sat there marveling at my good fortune, I could hear the sound of the Rio Grande flowing by. There were hawks hovering above and eventually my mind slowed down enough so that I could start to enjoy the pleasures of my surroundings. Looking up into a blue sky I remembered the night I had spent at the junction of the Pecos River and the Rio Grande and I thought: "this water will eventually meet at that very juncture," and I imagined being on a raft and letting the river take me to that very place. I had come such a long way from that night and had experienced so many adventures and here was just another adventure to try to assimilate. Eventually, the enjoyment ceased as thoughts of some authority discovering me sitting naked in the pool and threatening me. It still had not occurred to me that every time I was in a situation where I was enjoying myself the thoughts of a "boogeyman" would come up.

As a child living with a French Canadian Catholic family in Quebec with a seventeenth century Catholic belief system and speaking a seventeenth century French dialect, I grew up with many boogeymen. He was either the devil over my left shoulder and whispering naughty things to do that would upset my mother or he was the "bon homme sept heure", old man seven o'clock, my mother's version of the boogeyman. As a child living in Montreal I once had the experience of the "boogeyman." My older sister, Monique, and I had been warned not to play in the basement because the "bon homme sept heure" would get us. We later found out that the reason for not playing in the basement was because we never knew when the coal deliveryman would come by and dump coal down a chute through the basement window and possibly bury us if we were in the coal bin playing. I was maybe three years old and one day Monique and I were playing in the basement. Our basement was separated from the attaching basement by slats of wood with about an inch or two of space between the slats. While we were busy playing, someone in the other basement started hammering a piece of wood between the slats and we immediately thought it was the "boogeyman." We both ran out of there and up the stairs and outside so fast that I still remember it to this day. First of all I remember the fear that I felt. Secondly I remember how fast I moved. I was a chubby kid and nicknamed slowpoke by my family and at least for those moments, it didn't apply. So the "boogeyman" has stayed with me into my adult life and surfaces often when I'm enjoying myself.

This "man" my folks created for me was a pretty faithful watchdog.

Anyway after I got out of the hot spring I dipped myself into the cold Rio Grande. That was one of the most invigorating experiences my body ever had. Then I got dressed and walked back to the community in Arroyo Hondo. When the weekend arrived, I asked about going to the Lama Foundation and I was told that there wasn't much going on over there but that Sunday might be a good day to go.

Since Krishna wasn't feeling very well, I trekked up to the Foundation by myself. The road to the Foundation was not paved and frozen in some areas and quite muddy in other places where the sun was hitting the road. By now I had gotten used to the thinner air so the 8700-foot elevation didn't bother me. When I arrived, I was taken by how quiet the place was. There was just the sound of the wind whistling through the trees and birds doing their usual chirping and a few hawks flying around. I didn't see another human being for quite awhile until I knocked and entered the main building. A young woman of about twenty-five with long black hair, and a thin body wearing a loose fitting dress and obviously braless, greeted me. I'll call her Sita. She showed me around. Showed me the community bath. It was a blue tiled tub or pool, which probably could fit eight people comfortably. Just the thought of having a community bath with Sita was already in my imagination and a good reason for joining this community. She said that people were still dropping LSD on a regular basis and that there were no plans for any spiritual teachers until the Summer. There were plans to build some adobe meditation huts when the weather permitted and I was invited to join them in the construction. There were huge illustrations of Ram Das' book, Be Hear Now, around the main building and Sita referred to him with great reverence. After about two hours, I started back down the mountain towards Arroyo Hondo a bit disappointed that they were still doing acid and didn't find what I was looking for there. Not that I was clear about what I was looking for but as far as acid was concerned, as they say, "Been there, done that".

On my walk back I decided to spend a few more days with my new found friends in Arroyo Hondo then leave for Denver to see my daughter Michelle. I had already done LSD and was not interested in continuing that experiment. I always enjoyed the effect, but it was never long lasting and I wanted something a bit more concrete. In spite of my disappointment with the Foundation, I was enthusiastic about continuing on with my search.

Having gone to the Foundation on Sunday started to give me some sense of the days of the week passing. Up until then the days seemed to flow into the other without considering what day of the week it was. On Wednesday, I made plans to leave the community in Arroyo Hondo. I had looked at my map and decided to go back through Taos and then on to Eagle Nest by way of route 64 and eventually to highway I 25 towards Denver. Everyone told me that the best way was to take route 522 North from Arroyo Hondo and eventually make connections towards Denver. Although that route seemed more direct not only because of my friend's directions but according to the map, but my intuition (my gut I called it then) was very strong to go the "indirect way." And I may add that I didn't have a dime to my name. I had some snacks my friends had given me and some dry dog food for Krishna and a couple of joints.

So off we went hitchhiking towards Taos. It seems that people around there don't let you stand by the road for very long because I got a ride almost right away. The first ride asked me where I was going and when I said: "Denver", he said that I was going the wrong way. It's amazing that in spite of the fact that everyone seemed to be steering me in the opposite direction, my intuition stayed strong. Oh, I did have some glimpses of doubt but anyway I wasn't in a hurry. The first ride took me to route 64 in Taos, and as soon as I got out of the car I knew that I had made the right decision. Sometimes that feeling inside is so strong, you just can't ignore it. I must have walked about three miles with my thumb out when a man pulled up and offered me a ride. "Where are you going", he said. "I'm going to Denver by way of I 25." "Great. I'm on my way home to Texas and I have to cross I 25. I'll drop you off there."

This man was about fifty-five or so and he was returning from a fishing trip and was pleased to have a passenger to talk to and help keep him awake. The road from Taos to Eagle Nest is mountainous and winding and slow. He talked about his life and how stressful it was. About twice a year he took a trip by himself to regain some perspective.

He was married and its not that he didn't love his wife but once in awhile he just wanted to go off by himself and fishing was one of the ways that he did something for his peace of mind. I shared with him about my hitchhiking experience and we got along real well.

Also, he had a cooler in the back seat with cans of beer, bread, lunchmeat and mustard. When we started coming down the mountain towards Eagle Nest, the whole valley opened up to a most spectacular site. The town is situated on the stunning Enchanted Circle Highway at the Northern most tip of Eagle Nest Lake. We stopped for gas there and feasted on baloney sandwiches and beer. I guess you have to be in certain situationsto truly treasure that kind of a meal. I still remember that meal forty-nine years later.

After our feast, we continued on route 64 around the northern part of the lake and then up the mountain again. At Cimarron, New Mexico we turned onto state road 58 and east towards I 25. After crossing the overpass to the highway, I got out and walked down to the side of the road. I had a drink of water and as I was giving Krishna some water, I saw an orange VW on the horizon heading my way and something inside said:

"There's my ride." The VW went zooming past me and I turned to watch it disappear when it stopped under the overpass about a hundred yards away and started to back up towards me. It was a woman driving. She rolled down the window and asked where I was going and when I said: "Denver", she said that's where she was going and I could ride with her.

We got in the car and as we drove away she said: "I wanted to pick you up and then I thought "no" and then I saw your dog and I thought "anyone traveling with a dog can't be all bad. So I decided to stop and give you a ride. My name is Sandy by the way."

"Hi. I'm Andre and this is my dog, Krishna. Is your home Denver"?

"Yes it is. I'm just coming back from Santa Fe where I just finalized a divorce and I got a real good settlement and I feel so good."

"Congratulations. How long were you married'?

"We were married almost five years. It didn't work out, but we're still friends. I live up in Denver. He lives in Santa Fe where he works in his business. We still love each other but as a marriage it doesn't work out so he gave me a very good settlement."

"Good for you. Divorce doesn't usually end up that amiable."

Sandy asked me what I was doing and I told her about my journey up until now.

"I'm on my way to see my daughter in Denver for a few days then I'll be going to Minneapolis", I said. "By the way some of my friends in Arroyo Hondo gave me some pot as a going away gift. Would you like to smoke some"?

"Yeah. Let's celebrate."

I rolled up a joint and we got high in that little VW going north on I 25 on a partly cloudy day and I was feeling very lucky and appreciative. My good fortune up until now was more than I ever could have imagined. The feeling in my body that had been so constricted most of my life was starting to open up. A sense of connectedness with the Universe was starting to be felt and something inside was freeing up and it wasn't just the pot I was feeling. We stopped in Trinidad, Colorado for some lunch, which Sandy treated. She was genuinely happy that I was along especially when I offered to drive.

The rest of the drive to Denver was filled with talking about our individual lives. I talked at length about the book: Be Here Now and how that had become my bible. I offered to give it to her when we arrived in Denver. She mentioned that she had been taking another look at her life and how it wasn't going in the direction that she had imagined when she was growing up. We smoked liberal amounts of pot and Marlboros.

About five o'clock that afternoon she pulled into the parking lot of the apartment where Michelle was living. Sandy and I exchanged phone numbers and I knew that I would be getting in touch with her again. Definitely a lady that I wanted to further a relationship with.

When I knocked on Michelle's apartment door, I wasn't sure what to expect. She opened the door and there was a wonderful reception that was heartfelt. She said: "Hi daddy, I missed you so much." "I missed you too honey. Is your mom home yet"? "No. She'll be home soon after she's off work." Michelle and I were catching up on events when her mother walked in. She didn't seem that upset about seeing me and told me that she had a date for dinner and Michelle and I could manage. That was fine with me. Before she left on her date I told her that I would be there just a day or two and that I needed a pass from her to fly back to Minneapolis. Since we were not officially divorced yet, I still qualified for free passes on her airline. I also needed a kennel for Krishna and papers for the dog showing that she had her necessary shots. "And by the way", I said, "I'm broke but when I get back to Minneapolis I'll go back to teaching and send you the money". "Here we go again", she said with a look of disgust and weariness.

The next day I used her car to get shots for Krishna so that she could qualify for air travel. We got her a kennel and on Thursday I was on a flight to Minneapolis. After being on the road hitch hiking for about three weeks, it was a relief to fly again.

Elizabeth picked me up at the airport. Seeing her again and renewing our relationship was seamless and getting laid after more than three weeks was sweet. Although our physical relationship was renewed something was different. It seemed quite superficial. Something within me was still a bit restless and I could sense that this relationship wouldn't be enough for me. But for now it would do.

The day after arriving I called the Minneapolis school system and registered again as a substitute teacher. I started getting calls right away and here I was back to where I had left the December before. Something had changed, however. I had changed but not sure what the changes were, I just knew that I was different. I didn't have a car so I used Elizabeth's bike to get back and forth. I was now taking my life one day at a time with little anxiety about how things were going to turn out. At least I had shelter with a bed and a beautiful, young and sexy lady to share it with. My needs were pretty basic and I was cruising along until the morning when the phone didn't ring for a substitute teacher gig.

Having a day off gave me an opportunity to ride my bike over to the Augs-burg college campus, my alma mater, and check things out. I spent the day in the student coffee shop and hung out with students I still knew and a couple of teachers. As I was leaving to return home later that afternoon, the school paper had just been

ONE MAN'S SEARCH FOR THE DIVINE

placed by the exit and I picked up a copy. On the second to the last page, there was an ad that read: The devotees of Guru Maharaj Ji will be speaking Tuesday in the student lounge at 7:30 PM. As soon as I read the word "Guru", I became interested in the meeting. I remembered in the book Be Hear Now when he said: "You don't find the Guru, he finds you when you're ready."

I became very excited. This is the way it works. I'm getting closer, I told myself. You search and eventually you find what you're looking for. Isn't that what the scriptures say: "Ask and it will be given to you; seek and you will find; knock and the door will be opened to you. " Well, I've been seeking and asking. I guess the thing I hadn't done yet was to knock and it seemed that maybe I would find the right door to knock on or maybe it will be a buzzer.

I was so excited about this meeting coming up that when I got home I looked again at the school paper to make sure of the date and time. As I read the announcement again I also saw the address of the Ashram only six blocks away. So I walked down to the Ashram. It was a big two-story house on a corner lot. From the sidewalk, I walked up about a dozen steps to the front door and knocked. No answer. After a few minutes, I knocked again but there was no answer, so I tried the door. When it opened I stuck my head in and called out: "Is anybody home"? There was no answer. Then I did something out of character for me, I went around the back of the house and knocked on the door. As this is going on I'm becoming aware of observing my behavior. This isn't like me I thought. I'm not usually this assertive. When no one answered, I again tried the door.   It opened and I yelled out: "Is anyone home"? No answer. A feeling of delight in my chest became apparent as I walked away. Instead of feeling disappointed, I felt an enthusiasm that was rare for me. As I came back around to the front, a young man of about twentytwo was just getting out of his VW with some poster materials in his arms. He looked at me as I approached and I said: "That's it. That's what I want. I want that look you have in your eyes." "What", he said. "I want that look you have in your eyes. You know something and I want to know what that is." He nodded like he understood. He told me his name was John and invited me into the house. We removed our shoes before we entered. The entrance led immediately into a large living room totally void of furniture except one stuffed chair and pillows of all sizes scattered around the room. On one wall was a large picture of a young boy of Indian origin wearing a white pajama.

The eyes in the picture were looking right at me with the same look I had seen in my dream the month before. "This is the boy who came to me in a dream a month ago," I said to John. He seemed to understand and I shared some of my dream with him. As we were sitting there on the pillows talking, a young girl of about the same age seem to glide down the stairs with hardly any interruption and sat next to

John. She introduced herself as Jenny B. Good.

Honestly, that was her real name. She was petite with blue eyes and radiated energy that was peaceful, accepting, open and loving. When I asked about this young Indian boy, she said: "His name is Guru Maharaj Ji." "What does he do?" I asked. "He will show you God face to face."

I thought to myself: "That's a pretty outrageous claim to make. I've never heard anyone make such a claim." As she talked I felt more and more captivated by what she was radiating. It didn't sound like a sales pitch. It was very matter of fact. So I said: "How much does it cost?" By now I had pretty much paid for everything else. My college education had cost me a small fortune. The week prior I had gone to a lecture on Transcendental Meditation and was told that it would cost me $125 to get interviewed for a personal mantra. I wanted to know what "seeing God face to face" was going to set me back. "Oh", Jenny said, "You can't buy your way into this one. You have to come and ask with the heart of a child for this gift and if you are sincere then the experience that Maharaj Ji calls Knowledge will be revealed to you.

Everything I was being told started to resonate for me especially the part of "asking with the heart of a child" and "not being able to buy my way in". I started to think that the search that I had started after I left my wife, Carol, was not whimsy. "I'm getting closer and closer," I told myself. After about a half hour, I excused my-self and said that I'd be back. "We have satsang every night at seven if you want to come this evening you're welcome," John said. "What's 'satsang'? I asked. "They're spiritual discourses.

Discourses on the nature of Truth,", Jenny added. Again that resonated for me and I made an internal intention to return by seven. I walked back to the apart-ment brimming over with enthusiasm. My day was getting brighter with every step. When Elizabeth arrived from work I told her about the people at the ashram and what they had shared with me.

We had dinner and walked to the meeting to see what this Satsang thing was all about. When we arrived a few minutes before seven, the living room was already buzzing with people. There were about twenty-five or thirty people sitting on the floor or on pillows. John came in and sat facing us and closed his eyes to meditate. When he opened his eyes, it was obvious that he had experienced something during the brief period of time that he had his eyes closed because a huge smile appeared on his glowing face. He spoke about this boy Guru and how unique he was. He talked about how life had been for him before he met the Guru. Although he had what he considered a good life and loving parents, something was missing. College brought even more frustration for him and finally he dropped out. Somebody had told him to check out this Indian boy and John eventually "received Knowledge." Jenny was next to speak and she basically told the same story of dissatisfaction with her life and after searching found a teacher in this young Guru and also "received Knowledge." She said that she had never felt so fulfilled.

Another guy talked after that and he talked about how everything in his life was limiting. "You can do only so many drugs until it is no longer satisfying", he said. "Then all the other things I was addicted to eventually became disappointing." The last person who spoke was a guy. He talked about how he had been addicted to popcorn. He said: "Although I loved popcorn, I could eat only so much and then I'd be full. The longing or the hunger or the thirst that I was feeling inside could not be quenched by any of this stuff. And then Knowledge came along and that did it for me."

This guy I could definitely relate to, especially the popcorn part. I had such an addiction to popcorn that I would fantasize being in a small room filled with hot buttered popcorn with a beer tap in front of me and just eat popcorn and drink beer until I was totally satisfied. Not a fantasy I shared with many people until now. About an hour later the meeting was finished and we were all invited to return every night for satsang and told that soon there would be a Mahatma coming who had been delegated by the Guru to impart Knowledge and this was the guy to ask.

As Elizabeth and I walked home from the meeting I began to think that perhaps there was some validity to the feelings of dissatisfaction and discontent all these years. That I was not an emotional freak of nature after all. That there were others who were also searching for something more substantial in their lives. When I shared these thoughts with Elizabeth, she seemed less enthusiastic. Then she said that she wasn't sure about these people. In any case, she would continue to check it out along with me.

The following day I got a call from the Minneapolis substitute teacher office and was asked if I would consider going to sub at an inner city junior high school. The last time I had substituted there I came home that day a total wreck and I told the office to never send me there again. The lady on the other end of the line apologized but said that they couldn't find anyone who would be willing to go and asked if I would consider doing this as a courtesy to her. Something inside of me, that familiar voice again said: "Take it." So I took it. I sensed and unusual calm that morning and rode my bike to the school in high spirits. This junior high school was the type that as soon as the school bell rang, they locked the doors.

66

I was assigned a class on the second floor overlooking the asphalt playground. There was total chaos in the room when I entered. A male student was by an open window throwing paper airplanes out the window and watching them land in the yard. There was another male student in the far corner with his boom box on his shoulder and listening to music. There was another male at the front of the room writing on the blackboard with a screw. Chalks don't last very long in these schools. And two girls sitting at desks that they had arranged to face each other. They were playing a game of chicken with their hairbrushes. One girl would hit the other girl's knuckles until she said uncle and by then the knuckles would have red bloody dots. So this was the chaos I had walked into and I was surprisingly calm about the whole thing.

I saw myself observing this chaotic scene as a play and felt detached from it so I sat down on the teachers' desk facing the class and just watched to see what would happen. In the past, I would have added to the chaos by going around and ordering people to stop what they were doing: "You by the window stop doing that; turn that radio off and sit down; stop writing on the board and sit down; girls turn your chairs around and face the front of the room." By the time, you do this you have to start all over again and create much bedlam at the same time.

This time I had such an air of calmness, which by the way came effortlessly. Within a few minutes, in spite of the chaos, the students stopped doing what they were doing and sat in front of me becoming just as curious about me as I was about them. After introducing myself I told them that I had an assignment for them or we could do something else. "What's the something else," one of the female students asked? "You will know as soon as you make a decision, but it must be unanimous." "We'll take the something else," they all shouted out. I then proceeded to tell them about my trip starting from San Antonio all the way to Minneapolis.

They listened so attentively that they seem to have been transformed. They were no longer the threatening middle school inner city kids that I had experienced the first time I subbed at this school but a certain humanity had immersed. One boy asked: "Weren't you scared that somebody would hurt you or kill you?" "Yeah, I was scared. But it didn't happen. "One of the girls said: "Are you telling us that you slept outside most of the time." "That's right and it wasn't anything like what I had imagined." There were other questions at which time the bell rang for the end of the period and the students walked out calmly and thanked me. Apparently my story about my travels was such a hit that when the students for the next period arrived they wanted to hear all about it. When students got noisy or disruptive I didn't have to say anything because the other students shushed them. And so the rest of the day went by with little stress. I left that day with not only some new items for my bag of substitute teacher tricks but the realization that I had brought that peace and calmness with me

ONE MAN'S SEARCH FOR THE DIVINE

which is exactly what the Satsang message was the night before. I looked forward with enthusiasm to returning to the Ashram that evening.

The speakers from the previous night recommended that we attend satsang every night if we were sincere about receiving Knowledge and that way we would get clear about what was being offered. After a week of nightly Satsang, my daughter Michelle came to visit during her Spring break. She accompanied me on my evening satsang meetings.

One night at the meeting they showed a movie of Guru Maharaj Ji as a twelve year old in Delhi, India speaking to a group of people totaling over 100,000. In this movie, the young Guru said: "I declare I will establish peace in this world. But what can I do unless people come to me with a sincere desire in their hearts to know the truth?" Hearing this message increased my hope of finally finding someone who could show me something that wasfulfilling. As we were walking home from satsang, Michelle said to me: "Daddy I want this Knowledge." I said: "Fine. I'll get it and see what its like and then I'll help you get it." As I said earlier, Michelle was the only person in the world that I felt safe with and trusted. When she said that she wanted to have this Knowledge, it opened me up a little bit more. She left for Denver the next day.

The next night, at the ashram there was an announcement that a Mahatma was going to be arriving in a few days and this was the guy designated by Guru Maharaj Ji to give Knowledge. This was the guy I had to come and "ask with the heart of a child" for this gift of Knowledge. By now something had started to stir up between Elizabeth and I. Each night that I attended Satsang, I became more and more drawn in to the possibility of finally getting some practical answers for my life and as I was becoming more and more interested in this group she started seeing it as a cult. She had been going to meetings because I was going not because she was inspired to go. It had reminded me of our bicycle trip from San Antonio to The Lama Foundation which fizzled rapidly when the going got tough. It was OK with me that she wasn't on the same path or that she didn't even want my path. I didn't want her to get in my way or drag me down. And by now the whole sex thing, although it was a tempting lure, was no longer seductive enough to distract me from what I recognized as something I had been searching for all my life. Until then, I didn't know what that feeling of emptiness was telling me and besides I was always adept at numbing myself starting as a pre-schooler with sugar and later with wine and beer and sex. Eventually, the numbing became part of the legacy that I had inherited from my family and culture. In my late twenties and early thirties, I distracted myself from the painful feelings of despair and emptiness with psychedelics.

68

Andre Patenaude

Numbing was a common occurrence in my family and extended family, which totaled into the hundreds, what with my mother being one of twelve children and my father being from a family of six. In the nineteen forties Sunday afternoon get togethers with family usually consisted of the men sitting around in one room drinking beer, smoking and talking about the affairs of the world especially the state of the war while the women were in the other room talking about their kids or knitting or how to stretch a roast to last two or three days.

Men always had a particular smell to them. I was under the impression that "this is how men smell." Later on as I got older I realized that it was BO that I was smelling. The women always smelled like perfume mixed with the smell of mildew or mothballs. One smell that used to make me nauseous was that of some of my fat aunts. I always had to let them caress me across their bellies or their sweaty breasts and for me it was absolutely repulsive and to this day I associate fat women with that smell. And the kids, if they were old enough to walk or crawl, were off playing in whatever way their imaginations took them, but always making visits to the kitchen to size up the open beer bottles and taking occasional sips. It seems as though the adults never saw what was happening or they thought it was "cute." Sometimes I was lucky enough to be sitting on a certain uncle's lap who let me sip out of his glass of beer. Sometimes it was whisky and Seven-Up. That always took me by surprise and would often turn my legs into rubber.

Television was not available during WWII so entertainment was self-directed. There was an uncle with a large belly who wore suspenders. He had white thinning hair and usually had a day or two growth of salt and pepper beard. He also smelled like the rest of the men. He loved to play a game that I call: "jingling the coins." This was always a part of the family get together that I looked forward to. With a wide grin and a little bit inebriated, this uncle would find me and start jingling the coins in his pocket and that was the clue for me to initiate my part of this coin jingling game.

There was always this intense focus on the game. The jingling went on and on with no dialogue for a while. Then it was: "Serge do you want to see what I'm jingling." (My name at the time was Serge) And with great delight I would nod my head. Then uncle would take his hand out of his pocket with a huge mound of coins and he would ask: "do you want a nickel?" Nickels bought candy bars. Again I would nod. And he would say: "you pick out the nickel."

The Canadian nickels had eight edges to them and they had a bluish tint so it was easy for me to identify. I would pick out the nickel and run off and buy a candy bar at the local store. This game ended the day my mother overheard me ask for a nickel. "Don't give him that," she said to uncle. And proceeded to shame me for what

ONE MAN'S SEARCH FOR THE DIVINE

she thought was asking for money. She reminded me that "You don't ask, you wait until someone offers." After the shaming incident, I no longer played the game with uncle and spent a lot more time in the kitchen emptying beer bottles.

The Mahatma finally arrived one afternoon in mid March. His name was Mahatma Parlokanand. He was getting out of the car in front of the Ashram when I first saw him dressed in his saffron robes with a shaved head and a red dot on his forehead. He looked like he was in his early twenties. My friends at the Ashram gathered around him along with those traveling with him and made this huge fuss. He looked into my eyes from a distance and I felt totally exposed and shut down. I thought to myself: "This is the loving saint that they were all praising about?" I felt no love at all. I was totally shut down and withdrawn and put off by what I thought was an outrageous and inappropriate display of affection. What saved me at the time was feeling my heart still longing for some relief and also sensing that what these people were telling me could help me. Little by little I was learning to trust my heart. We were told to come back that evening at seven for Satsang with Mahatma Ji.

That night Elizabeth and I went back to the Ashram to listen to the Mahatma. There were about seventy to eighty people there. Some people had followed him from New York to Detroit to Chicago to Madison Wisconsin to Minneapolis. He spoke and quoted past Masters such as Kabir, Jesus, and Krishna. He told many stories from different scriptures such as the Bhagavad-Gita, the Vedas, and the Bible. While he spoke I started to thaw a little bit from the emotionally frozen state I found myself after the initial meeting early on that day. I was told that when the seeker starts to get close to finding God then the mind starts its battle with the person. Until then, the mind pretty much has an exclusive on that person. I was starting to feel some of the battles that I had heard about.

My heart was saying yes and my mind was judging and criticizing the Mahatma and my friends in the Ashram. Paranoia started to materialize its ugly head again and I became confused and ungrounded. At the end of the night, we were invited to return the next evening again for Satsang and if we wanted we could participate in the ritual of singing Aarti, a devotional song to the living Master. Personally I had had enough and so had Elizabeth. I could already feel my mind squirming and I felt extremely uncomfortable. Even so I was determined to return the next evening. With some reluctance, Elizabeth accompanied me to the Ashram the next night. When we arrived the room was almost full and my friends invited us to sit on pillows next to the speaker's chair. I was instructed by them again that if I wanted to receive Knowledge that I would have to ask the Mahatma directly. After a couple of the local Ashram residents spoke we were introduced to Mahatma Parlokanand. He sat in the chair for a few minutes with his eyes closed. When he opened his eyes he looked around the

70

room and acknowledged some of the people with a nod then he looked at me and I got on my knees, put my hands together and put on my best show of piety and said: "Mahatma Ji will you please give me this Knowledge?" "How long have you been listening to Satsang," he asked? I thought for a few seconds and realized that I had been seeking God my whole life. I decided to be clever and I answered: "thirty two years." Boy was that the wrong answer. He replied: "Thirty-two years. That's very good. Guru Maharaj Ji has been in this country for two years and you've been listening to this Satsang for thirty-two years, that's very good." From that moment on he ignored me and fielded a request from someone else in the room who also was asking for Knowledge. I remained frozen on my knees with embarrassment and didn't hear a word he said for the rest of the night.

How dare he treat me this way I thought to myself. How can he treat people like this and expect them to stick around? I was seething with anger and frozen to the floor on my knees with embarrassment.

Fortunately, my heart was in the thawing stage and very much alive because I simultaneously knew that I was being "tested." My adult self was still very much in charge. When the Satsang was finished, we were again invited to return the next morning at ten to continue with Mahatma Ji and we could stay to sing Aarti before we left but I declined. As we exited the Ashram the premies had started singing and I could feel a glow of warmth and love emanating from the house. Elizabeth and I walked home in silence as I had a lot to process.

My heart was starting to take over and my mind was getting stronger. I had read in one of the books, which talked about the search for God, that when a human being gets closer and closer to experiencing God, the mind starts to become more and more resistant. It is described as a wild animal being cornered and it is fighting for its freedom.

The mind does not want to be controlled. It just wants free reign to do whatever it wants to do. And I was starting to see how much my mind had been in charge of my life so far and not doing such a good job of it. However it could only do what it had been programmed to do and it was filled with programmed ignorance. Elizabeth was angry about the way I had been treated and told me that she was not interested in continuing on with "this whole cult thing." I told her that I understood what was going on and that I was okay with it.

The next morning I arrived at the Ashram fifteen minutes early and I was the first one there. The residents were still eating breakfast and there was an air of ease in the house. I was offered something to eat, but I declined. They told me that

ONE MAN'S SEARCH FOR THE DIVINE

the Mahatma was out doing a radio interview but would return in a little while and to find a pillow and sit wherever I wanted. So I sat next to his chair. By the time eleven came around the room was packed with the same familiar faces that I had seen the two previous days. We all sat in the room and waited for the Mahatma while some of the residents were sharing their experience of searching for God or Truth or whatever they were calling the object of their search. I kept thinking that I didn't care about their search, I was told to come back this morning to listen to the Mahatma and ask him for Knowledge and he hasn't shown up yet and it's almost noon. I was starting to get really annoyed with these people. They were so unprofessional about the way that they went about things. This is just not the way to get things done: not showing up on time, no apologies, no consideration, no catering to my ego needs. How can these people expect anyone to put up with the way that they do things? And all this time my heart is saying just be patient.

Finally, a little bit after noon the Mahatma comes in with some of the premies that had accompanied him and sat down on an empty chair next to me. No apologies for making us wait. A few minutes later I said to Parlokanand: "Mahatma Ji will you give me this Knowledge please?" He looked at me for a few minutes as if he didn't hear my request and he said: "I want you to shave your face." Boy did that throw my mind for a loop. I had been told that all I had to do was to come and ask "with the heart of a child" and here I'm being told to shave. And besides I've been growing this beard now for about a month and it's looking good, and what does one thing have to do with the other so I said:

"Why?"

"What?" Parlokanand said.

"Why do I have to shave my beard?"

"You don't argue with Mahatma Ji, you do what Mahatma Ji tells you."

And then he ignored me and started answering questions from others in the room. Again this guy embarrasses me in front of all these people and again I felt frozen but this time on my ass, not on my knees. I couldn't even leave the room because there are all these people between the door and myself. So I just sat there like a bump on a log seething with embarrassment and contempt. After about an hour of answering questions, a break was announced. I was finally able to stand up from my frozen position with a confused look on my face and I was not a happy camper.

When John saw my state of mind he said: "André he's just testing you. He just wants to find out what's going on with you, where you're coming from." As I heard that I was able to start breathing again. Every muscle in my body began to relax and I knew in my heart that he was telling me the truth. "In that case, I'm going to shave," I said. "You can shave right here right now if you want," John said. He walked me to the bath room and brought a pair of scissors, some shaving cream and a razor. The bathroom door stayed open while Jenny, whom I had met on the first day at the Ashram, cut my beard. When she was finished, I lathered up and began shaving while another Ashram resident with a guitar sang some spiritual songs in the hallway by the bathroom. There was such a buzz of celebration while I was shaving and the feelings of love were so powerfully felt that I started to cry and the tears were forming trails through the shaving cream. I wasn't sure what was happening except that I felt safe and loved and there was literally a warm glow everywhere. After the break, we went back to our pillows in the hall for another hour of Satsang. At about five, we were told to return at seven for more Satsang and possibly a selection for the Knowledge session. The "Knowledge session" continued to be a mystery to me and I couldn't imagine what they meant. I walked home with a spring in my gait feeling light and enthusiastic.

When I got home and shared with Elizabeth my experience and the possibility of going back later for another Satsang session, she seemed less than supportive and enthusiastic for me. I think she probably sensed that she was losing me to as she calls it this "sect." Elizabeth indicated that she would not accompany me that evening and that she would see me when I got home.

My walk back to the Ashram after dinner was filled with all kinds of questions: Could this be what I've been looking for all my life; is this Knowledge what Ram Das was describing in his book Be Here Now. At least it wasn't going to cost me anything. When I walked into the Ashram after taking off my shoes, there was a buzz I had not felt up until now. The room was lit with candles and the Ashram residents seemed to be radiating with light and love. The smiles on their faces and the sparkle in their eyes seemed genuine. The gentleness and kindness with the way they treated everybody was so obvious. They made sure that we all had pillows to sit on. Water was offered. And instructions on how to ask the Mahatma for Knowledge were given very explicitly: 'Mahatma Ji, May I have this Knowledge please?" At seven, the hall was packed like sardines when the Mahatma walked in.

He spoke about the love of the Perfect Master and the gift of Knowledge that he revealed. There was talk of grace and how past Masters had imparted this Knowledge since the beginning of humanity.

There were many quotes from the Vedas, the Baghavad Gita, the Ramayana

ONE MAN'S SEARCH FOR THE DIVINE

and the Bible. Other past Masters were quoted. As he spoke, I could feel something within me stirring that I recognized as hope. After about an hour, Mahatma Parlokanand took a short break. He came back with one of the Premies who had accompanied him from city to city. With Parlokanand standing next to him he said: "Mahatma Ji has decided that he is going to give Knowledge to fifteen people." As soon as this announcement was made, people around me started to jump up and down yelling: "Pick me Mahatma Ji, pick me." I was standing in front of Parlokanand and he would point to one person and then another and it seemed that he was looking all around me but ignoring me. And of course I wasn't jumping up and down. That part of me that was still stuck in behaving like an adult which was still very much in charge. While everyone was jumping up and down and yelling, I had one arm half raised with the other arm holding it back and trying to act "respectful and polite." And besides I didn't follow him from city to city so I probably didn't deserve to be chosen. I hadn't been "listening to Satsang" as long as the others had.

So far the adult in me is winning and my inner child is being held down. They were a lot more deserving than I to be selected. So being passed by was just logical. When the fifteenth person was selected and I wasn't one of them, I thought to myself: " I'm going to follow you until you give me this Knowledge. I can leave Elizabeth again after all I left my wife and daughter to search for that missing piece in my life I can do it again." While I'm going through this thought process, I heard a Premie say: "Mahatma Ji is so merciful and so kind and so loving" and while he's saying this I'm thinking: "He's just fucking with our minds," "that he's going to choose five more for the Knowledge session." When I heard this, something inside finally broke loose. It didn't matter that I had walked just seven blocks when most of the others had been driving from city to city. It was as if someone had walked into a room full of five year olds with one popsicle and asked: "who wants a popsicle?" If I'm truly faithful and true to my inner child, I'm not going to analyze the situation by thinking that there are other kids more deserving than me or that someone's feelings will be hurt if they don't get the popsicle. No. The honest thing is that I want it. It has nothing to do with who is more deserving. So my hand raised straight up over my head and I jumped up and down with the heart of a child and said: " me Mahatma Ji, pick me. Look I shaved like you asked, choose me." And Parlokanand pointed to me and said: "you." I was so happy and a bit stunned. I wouldn't have to follow him around after all but a nagging part of me kept thinking that he had made a mistake. "He doesn't really know whom he's chosen, " I thought. "If he really got to know me he never would have chosen me. Here I am this thirty-two year old pseudo hippie addicted to drugs, alcohol and sex. Anything that will numb the pain that was so much a part of my life and yet I've been chosen to receive this most precious of all gifts which all the money in the world can't even buy. I was also very humbled to have been chosen. In spite of

Andre Patenaude

he shame that I was harboring, I had been chosen. We were instructed to go home and take a bath and clip our fingernails and return at two the following morning. The Knowledge session would last about four hours.

I went skipping home and rode the wave of having been chosen. Again Elizabeth wasn't very enthusiastic about me being chosen for the Knowledge session. I told her about the instructions I had been given and decided to sleep on the couch that night so that I wouldn't disturb her when I got up and also so I could sleep undisturbed. Did I say sleep undisturbed? I was so buzzed about going to the Knowledge session that sleep was hard to find. That familiar non-verbal voice that I had "heard" so many times when I was hitchhiking called me to itself and I fell asleep. I woke up at one thirty AM refreshed, shaved, bathed and manicured. It was April 3rd 1973. I briskly walked to the Ashram in the cool night air barely touching the sidewalk. I felt like Gene Kelly in the movie Dancing in the Rain just tapping down the street.

When I arrived at the Ashram, there was a glow in the house. The familiar pairs of shoes were all placed neatly by the front door. I was greeted by John and Jenny and escorted to a room upstairs lit only by candlelight. It was a hard wood floor with twenty pillows arranged in two rows of ten. In the front of the room there was an altar with a picture of Guru Maharaj Ji on the wall. Since I was one of the first ones there I took a pillow in the front row. The rest of the aspirants (that's what we were called) arrived in the room over a period of time and at about fifteen minutes past two the Mahatma arrived in his Sunday best saffron clothes. He had a red Tilak on his forehead and was all smiles and kindness. The room was glowing with warmth. I saw him in a way that I had not seen him until this moment. The love and care for me that seemed absent in the past were now very present. I felt very well taken care of and my whole body relaxed. We were all in a state of anticipation.

The Mahatma welcomed us all and began reading from various scriptures that related to the Knowledge he was about to reveal. He said that this Knowledge was the Raj Vidya, meaning the Knowledge of Knowledges or the King of Knowledges. The more he spoke the more excited I got. Oh my God, I'm in a very select group, I thought. I was ready to achieve Sainthood on the spot. I was imagining myself totally transformed by the time I walked out of the room. I can't wait, I thought. According to him, all he was going to do was show us four different techniques and the experience we were to have was by the "grace of Guru Maharaj Ji." He said that he was just a channel for the "Grace." I kind of understood that and anxious to see how that worked. After about a half hour of quoting scriptures from different texts from around the world and speaking about "this precious gift" we were about to receive, he told us that we had to promise three things before we received Knowledge. The first thing was to promise to practice one hour a day.

75

ONE MAN'S SEARCH FOR THE DIVINE

The second was to promise to stay in touch with Guru Maharaj Ji and the third promise was to never reveal the techniques to anyone. Each one of us made the promises and the ceremony started. We were all told to close our eyes and the first technique would be revealed and to practice the technique for thirty minutes. After we had finished practicing the first technique we were asked by the Mahatma about our experience. Some of the aspirants talked about seeing white light others saw colored lights or donuts of light and "how incredible it was." I lied. Because my experience was particularly frustrating and I didn't want to appear to have missed the experience so I described an experience I once had on Mescaline. So much for remaining "like the heart of a child." I think a child would have said: "I didn't see anything." But now I had to impress people by how evolved I was.

Then the second technique was revealed and I lied about my experience on that also by the time the third technique was going to be revealed, I was starting to feel pretty disappointed and wondered if I was just missing the boat or if I was being totally conned by this whole thing. Conned by my friends John and Jenny B. Good Conned by the hype of this Mahatma and other premies that I had heard speak for the last few weeks. I remembered being hyped as a six year old about how wonderful it would be going to school, and after one day I never wanted to go back because the teachers were so mean and abusive in this all boys Catholic elementary school. And I was starting to feel really, really depressed on a day when I was, according to my expectations, going to walk out of this Ashram a saint after having realized God. I did stay long enough for the third technique, however. I had nothing to loose. I can't ask for my money back, there's no money involved. "I can't buy my way into this," I was told.

The third technique was revealed and this time I experienced something that was very familiar. It was an experience that I used to have when I received Communion, especially as a young child. When I was being prepared for my First Communion in the first grade I was told that I would be receiving Jesus in this host, a small round piece of white flat, thin bread. And I believed those instructions, so when I received my First Communion at the age of seven, I came back to my pew, knelt down, bowed my head toward my heart and prayed to Jesus who was right there in my stomach. The feeling that I always had was of peace, joy, and a loving presence that I thought was Jesus. That feeling was there every time I received Communion. And here it was again as I practiced the third technique. I couldn't believe that all this time that feeling that I felt when I received Communion had always been there and no one ever told me. It had nothing to do with receiving Communion. It had nothing to do with that little piece of bread. The experience of peace and love and joy had always been there inside my own heart and I was totally ignorant of it. How simple it was. Of

76

course, I was familiar with this feeling but I didn't know that this was God that I was feeling. It was too simple, too subtle. It wasn't anything like the experiences on acid or mescaline or psilocybin. This third technique wasn't blasting me with an experience. It wasn't blowing my circuits. It was so subtle and sweet. I was now starting to feel a bit more encouraged to continue.

Then the fourth technique was revealed and again it was a major disappointment. By the time this whole ceremony was finished, I was almost in a state of shock. I wasn't going to walk out of this place a saint. I wanted something similar to my mescaline experience when I saw a light that was blissful, loving and so exhilarating that it lasted for weeks. I wanted to merge with that light and shockingly disappointed by this Knowledge experience. I had not experienced God according to my expectations, but I did think that I had experienced the ultimate hype.

At the end of the Knowledge session, we were invited to have breakfast with those premies living in the Ashram. I wanted to leave because I was angry and stunned, but I figured I might as well get a breakfast out of it. Everyone at the breakfast table seemed to be in a festive mood. I was in a mood all right, but it wasn't festive. I was very quiet and somber while I was eating my granola and milk. I couldn't wait to get out of there and run home. I didn't want to talk to these people, which I felt had deceived me. So on my way home I made the decision to check out the meditation that my friend Carl was doing at the Buddhist center.

The following day I called Carl and we made arrangements to go to the Buddhist center where he would introduce me to his teacher. On our way there, I was still feeling the same mood that I had felt when I left the Ashram after the Knowledge session. I was still in a bit of a fog. The material world around me seemed surreal and it seemed like I was just floating on some current of energy. When we arrived at the Buddhist center, I was introduced to Carl's teacher. He asked me if I had had other meditation teachers in the past year and I told him that I had just been initiated in the Knowledge of Guru Maharaj Ji the week before but that I was not satisfied. He said that perhaps it would be best if I tried out the meditation for a few months and then make a decision. I wasn't very pleased with his answer and left the center disappointed and I was starting to get very irritated. As I left I decided to check out Transcendental Meditation again. After all that was something that I could buy my way into, I thought.

The next day I called the Transcendental Meditation center and asked if I could make an appointment to learn TM. I also asked if I could have a student rate since I didn't have much money. They asked me if I was a student I told them that I was a substitute teacher. They said that I would have to pay the non-student rate of one hundred and twenty five dollars. I told them that I only had enough money for the student rate of fifty dollars and I would be willing to give them that. They told me to save up and when I could afford the higher rate to call them back and to be free of drugs legitimate or otherwise for thirty days and that meant no pot. Well, I'll tell you that I dropped that idea like a hot potato. I was starting to feel very frustrated at not getting my way. I couldn't even buy my way into TM. So the idea of becoming a saint at least at the time started to fade away. Pot and acid became my choice of paradise again and I was willing to forget the whole thing.

About two weeks later I didn't get a call for a substitute assignment so I went to my alma mater, Augsburg College, and hung out in the coffee shop. After a couple of hours of hanging out, I dropped in to see John Mitchell my writing teacher. We talked about poetry and how this art form was so therapeutic for him and how he re-ferred to poetry to process his deep feelings. Eventually, it got around to John asking me how I was doing and I told him about my trip through San Antonio and how I got back to Minneapolis and finding this Guru and how disappointed I was with the initiation and the whole organization. Basically I was nya, nya-ing all over his desk. Then he stopped me abruptly and said: "Do you know what's wrong with you?" I automatically responded: "no." John said: "You have no devotion. You leave your wife and child, search for a teacher, you find him and he accepts you as a student he teaches you and initiates you and you leave him. You don't even give him a chance. Stay with him for a year at least. You've sacrificed too much to give up now." As he was talking, I thought to myself: "John, you have no idea that you are channeling the truth right now. You're telling me exactly what I need to hear." I was grateful for what John said to me and thanked him and left.

That night, Elizabeth and I had invited guests for dinner and I was to prepare it. It was to be a meatless meatloaf. As I was preparing it, anxiety began to overtake me and I became extremely uncomfortable. Perhaps practicing some of the Knowl-edge techniques I had learned would help, so I went into the bedroom and started to practice and within about ten minutes I started to feel a calmness and inner peace I had not felt in a long time and the longer I practiced the deeper the peace became. I felt so good about myself for having had the good sense to respond to my needs the way I did and felt grateful for what John Mitchell had shared with me that day. I knew that not getting the call to teach, and going to Augsburg and talking to John and being open to the wisdom that he shared with me was no accident. Just as this whole journey up until now was not an accident.

There was a synchronicity in my life that I just couldn't deny or ignore. After experiencing the deep peace from practicing the techniques of Knowledge, I went back to the food preparation and the sense of being in the here and now became a reality for the first time. I now understood on a feeling level what I had been reading about in Ram Das' book Be Here Now.

Everything I had read about the Masters and their teachings I wasexperiencing and it was nothing like what I had imagined. And certainly nothing like taking acid, or the other hallucinogens. There was no instant high, just a constant calmness and peace with a clarity that was joyous.

When Elizabeth came home from work that night, I was happy to see her in a way that I had never felt before and when her friend, Beth arrived with her boyfriend for dinner, everything was ready and we all had a warm and intimate evening together. This had been a going-away dinner for them a few days before they moved to Spearfish, South Dakota. Little did I know that, within a month, I would be spending a few days with them in their new home.

On the early morning of May 15th Elizabeth drove me and Krishna to highway 169 just southwest of Minneapolis and we said good-by. It wasn't a final good-bye just until we saw each other again. My plans were to return to the Lama Foundation and help with the construction of the adobe meditation huts. I had also planned to go to Spearfish, South Dakota and visit Beth and her boyfriend and then on to Denver and visit my daughter, Michelle. Standing on the side of the highway with my back pack and Krishna (the splint removed) with my thumb sticking out was not a new experience. What was new about it, however, was the feeling that I had. I no longer felt alone. I was with me now. Not the ego me which we often identify with and spend most of our lives trying to protect, but the sense of me. That feeling is always familiar because it had been there since the beginning of my life and never boring. Whenever I tune into the feeling of that presence within me which I call Divine, it's always seems new and refreshing and constant. No longer was I searching. I had found what I was looking for and now I could enjoy just being with me, free of anxiety and confusion. I don't know how others saw me, but it seemed to me that I had a grin that wouldn't quit. The feeling reminded me of a story I often heard at theSatsang sessions while preparing to have this Knowledge revealed to me. The story is about the Musk Ox who wanders around looking for the source of fragrance emanating from his navel.

The Ox never realizes that the fragrance is coming from his own body and he searches and searches looking for the source of the fragrance. And as human beings we do something similar. We search and search for the source of satisfaction and fulfillment outside of ourselves and it is already within us. We want the search to be complicated, yet it is subtle and simple. It blows me away how simple it is.

ONE MAN'S SEARCH FOR THE DIVINE

Another thought that occurred to me while standing by the road was that if this experience was so simple, why didn't my parents know about it. After all a formal education was not necessary to have this experience. Also, the priests, teachers, the Ph.Ds who were my teachers at Augsburg didn't know about it. The fact that what I was looking for was within me was not new information, it was in many of the books that I read but it seems passed over and my guess is that no one that I had met up until now knew how to look within for that treasure. I felt so fortunate to have finally found myself. Within about a half hour after being dropped off by Elizabeth, a VW van with a couple of hippies stopped and inquired as to my destination. When I mentioned Spearfish he told me to hop in. He was going as far as the Badlands and he would take me that far.

About an hour later they stopped and picked up another hitchhiker, a young guy of about twenty –two, who was also going to Spearfish. I'll call him Harry. Of course as was the custom we all got stoned. Around five, the driver pulled over and dropped us off just at the entrance to theBadlands National Park. Harry and I decided to camp out for the night and resume our trip the following day. We set up our sleeping bags on a bank on the side of the road.

I had my usual carrots and peanut butter for dinner and I fed Krishna her dog food. When it started to get dark and it does get very dark when city lights don't interfere. The heavens shyly and subtly began to display her cosmic creative juices of twinkling lights. As I lay on my back in my sleeping bag, totally absorbed and enchanted by the stars, it seemed as though the night sky got brighter and brighter. I was spellbound. I was totally consumed by the night sky and forgot that I had a body and became one with the universe, then sleep took over.

Sometime during the middle of the night, perhaps around two, the wind started to kick up and then the clouds blocked out the stars and the rain followed. Yes, the rain again.

Fortunately there was a huge billboard about fifty yards away and we rushed towards it for shelter. It was on an angle which blocked out the wind and the rain. We felt lucky. I rolled out my ground cloth and my sleeping bag on top of it and watched as Krishna scooted her way into the bag ahead of me. As my head touched the sleeping bag I felt relieved, I heard my mind say: "Ha ha ha you just outsmarted Mother Nature."

I said: "Yes I did" and immediately the wind shifted bringing the rain and my sleeping bag started to get wet. I flashed on what it was like when I was biking across Texas and getting rained on and feeling miserable. Something happened at that moment which is difficult to make sense of. I felt like a five-year old lost in the wilderness and broke down and cried out: "Please, please make it stop. This is really bumming me out." Immediately the wind stopped and the rain stopped and the clouds disappeared. I heard my mind again say: "Wow what a coincidence." And I knew that this was no coincidence. I began speaking to God. "You would do this for me? Who am I that You would do this for? Maybe there are people who really need the rain." Now I'm feeling very humbled, very much taken care of and very much loved and in a place of total acceptance of this Divine gift and totally free of doubt.

Then I heard in a voice that isn't English or French or words at all but more like being shown: "All you needed to do was to become like a little child and ask. All you needed was the faith of a mustard seed." Then when I realized the state of mind I was in when I begged for the storm to stop, I was like a little child. I wasn't this strong, macho thirty-two year old man. I drifted off to sleep feeling like I was in a warm womb and protected from all harm.

The following morning we woke up to a beautiful spring morning with clear skies and a light breeze. I felt light and still very much humbled from the "miracle" of the previous night. I had my usual breakfast of carrots and peanut butter and fed Krishna. Harry and I went back to the side of the road and started hitchhiking. So far I had kept my miracle to myself.

The traffic was a bit slow as we walked alongside the road with our thumbs pointing out. It wasn't tourist season yet and the RV's that drove by just waved at us and we waved back. About two hours later I started to think to myself about the storm and how suddenly it had stopped. I also wondered if maybe what I had done to bring on this "miracle" would work again. So I said: "We are really at your mercy Lord. The only way we are going to get from here to Spearfish is if You bring us a ride because we don't have any power to make anyone stop. All we can do is stick out thumbs out and let people know that we need a ride." Within a minute, some hippie was coming down the road in his white station wagon with the windows rolled down doing about thirty-five miles an hour and stopped. "Where are you guys going?" he asked. "Were going to Spearfish" we answered. "That's where I'm going. Hop in." Harry hopped in the front and I hopped in the back seat with Krishna and this hippie's dog. Now I'm really feeling blissed out.

Could all this really be going on and why is it so hard to accept? Why is my good fortune so difficult to believe. That's when I shared with Harry about what I did when the storm hit us in the middle of the night. "I wondered why the storm ended

ONE MAN'S SEARCH FOR THE DIVINE

so abruptly," he said. The rest of the ride was without much conversation. When we arrived in Spearfish, the driver dropped me off at Beth's place and I expected the car, the hippie driver and Harry to disappear in a puff of smoke like in a fairy tale.

Seeing Beth and her boyfriend Brad again was delightful. They had converted a school bus into a spare bedroom where Krishna and I were lodged. We spent the next two days smoking pot and hiking in the surrounding hills and talking about our adventures. Brad and Beth were fascinated by my adventures in my search for a Master and my initiation. When I told them about the "miracle" of the storm and my hitch hiking prayer, they found it hard to believe.

After a couple of days in Spearfish, I was ready to hit the road again. It was arranged that Beth and Brad would drop me off on the highway at the edge of town towards Denver and I would hitch hike. Since I now had hair down to my shoulders and a beard again, they warned me that it wasn't very safe for me. "There are cowboys around here that would just love to pick you up and tar and feather you" Brad said. "Maybe it would be safer if you shaved and cut your hair before you go out there." "I'm not afraid. I'm well taken care of. I'll be fine." I replied. This whole belief that rednecks and cowboys hating hippies to the degree that they wanted to tar and feather me never proved itself.

Before I moved to Texas I had heard these stories about rednecks mostly from Northeners and now I'm hearing similar stories about cowboys. It seems to me that we all seem pretty good at creating bad guys in our own minds and projecting them out there and maybe with enough conviction that inevitably bad guys do show up. Anyway I wasn't afraid and for the first time was free of paranoia. I felt freed up of more than just paranoia. Something within my physical and emotional body felt expanded and light. I was resonating joy, enthusiasm with a childlike quality.

On our way out of town towards U. S. highway 14, we stopped first at a diner for some breakfast. While we're eating breakfast, friends of Brad walked in with people he didn't know and sat in the booth next to us. So Brad asked his friend if he knew of anyone going to Denver today because I was needing a ride. His friend said that the people he was having breakfast with were leaving for Denver after they finished eating. So Brad asked if there was room for me and my dog and my backpack and of course there was room. I'm sitting there wondering to myself about this incredible string of luck I'm having and felt completely in sync with the Universe. Synchronicity was happening in front of my eyes and again because of my new felt sense of inner stillness, I could accept my good fortune and feel the grace along with it. The Universe is either hostile or benevolent depending on how I look at it. It is said that how you look at something changes what you look at. And I was starting to see the Uni-

82

verse as loving and benevolent, radically different from the way I experienced God or the Universe as a child.

There was a paradigm shift happening. A new reality was being experienced and it was wonderful and freeing. When it came time to leave the restaurant, I was introduced to the people giving me a ride: Larry and his wife Diane, their son, James and their dog. Their station wagon was pretty well packed but fortunately there was enough room for me and Krishna in the back seat with James and his dog. My backpack was secured to the roof along with other baggage. As the ride went on, I learned that they were also going to New Mexico but planning an overnight in Denver. It turned out to be a quiet ride and I took advantage of the stillness to take a nap.

We arrived in Denver around seven PM and I called a contact that I had gotten from John at the Minneapolis Ashram. It was a strange time for me because it seemed that everything I did was new and crisp. There was a certain surrender about my destiny that was totally free of worry and anxiety. I knew somehow that I would be taken care of and with that consciousness I called Speedy, my Denver contact. When Speedy answered the phone, I said: "Hi my name is André, I'm a Premie (someone who received Knowledge) and I just arrived from Minneapolis and was given your name as a cotact. I just arrived in town and need a place to crash.""Who gave you this contact" Speedy asked?"John at the Minneapolis Ashram.""Do you need directions to get here?""Yes I do. I'll get the driver and you can give it to him."

After Larry got the directions, I got back on the phone."The people who gave me a ride are on their way to New Mexico, but they need a place to crash for tonight. Is there room for them?""How many are there?""There's Larry and his wife and son."

"That's okay," Larry said.

"They also have a dog."

"That's okay."

"I also have a dog."

"Okay."

"Then we should be there in about twenty minutes."

"Have you and your friends had dinner," Speedy asked?

"No."

ONE MAN'S SEARCH FOR THE DIVINE

"We'll have soup for you when you get here. But we don't have dog food."

"That's all right, Speedy, we have dog food."

When I hung up and got back in the car, it felt like I was in a different world. Speedy didn't know me from Adam. Here I am a stranger in a strange City and unannounced until now with a car full of people I hardly know and two dogs and we're all welcome to this house for the night. Again as before with this great luck there was a feeling of acceptance, humility and gratitude. Feelings that had been rarely felt in my life, and bestof all my mind was still.

When we arrived at the house on Adams Street in Denver, we were met by Speedy, a redheaded Irishman with a gracious and mellow disposition. I wondered for a brief moment how he got labeled "Speedy." Larry and his wife were directed to a spare bedroom with foam pads on the floor which served as beds. James, their son and I and the two dogs were shown a space in the basement between the heater and the water heater. We were told to use our sleeping bags for the night. Once we settled down then we were invited to dine on homemade lentil soup anhome made bread.

Most of the occupants in this four bedroom duplex were students of the Guru and attending Satsang at a hall in downtown Denver and by the time they came back home around ten o'clock, we were all asleep.

The following morning, after a breakfast of scrambled tofu, I bid farewell to Larry, Diane and James. I made arrangements with Speedy to stay for awhile and paid for my room and board accordingly.

The "Premie house" as it was called had six people living there. A very diverse group of people from all parts of the United States. There was Chuck from Maine who had just gotten out of prison for cocaine possession and sales. He had been initiated by the Guru prior to prison and talked about his experience meditating in prison. I liked Chuck right away because he was outspoken and didn't have a pious bone in his body. We would eventually become good friends. And of course there was Speedy, a carpenter from Ohio and the house "father." There was Amy from California and still very much a hippie wearing a loose dress and hairy legs with a bush of hair under each arm, she was the house "mother" and the cook. There were others in the house whose names I don't remember who were doing service at the local headquarters, called Divine Life Mission.

After a few days and getting oriented to my new surroundings, I was told that Guru Maharaji had arrived in town and we could probably see him if we went and stood outside the residence where he was staying on Race Street. Someone gave me

84

a ride to the house. When I arrived, there were about a dozen people hanging around outside all waiting for the Guru's arrival.

What happened next I never could have prepared for. I had been told that this young fifteen year old Guru incarnated as a Master similar to Jesus. He also had been given the title of "Lord of the Universe." Some people considered him an Avatar and others considered him a God. Others saw him as their heavenly father. You can imagine the concepts floating around in my head by now. As I'm observing this whole scene of people quietly milling around, a red Ferrari drove up and parked along the curb in front of the house. The young fifteen year old Guru came out of the driver's door and walked by the front of the car near where I was standing and briefly made eye contact with me and within seconds he was inside the house leaving the people who had been waiting to see him prostrated on the ground. My impression at the moment was of someone who had his life together and although I had a college education and seventeen years older, I felt like a child and he was the adult. I had never met anyone who seemed so together let alone a fifteen year old. He resonated absolute self-assurance and unfazed by the bizarre activities around him.

As I was standing there talking to myself and saying: "This is the guy. This is the one they call "Lord." This is the one that is like Jesus." He had just walked by me and I didn't feel a thing. He hadn't said "Hi" to me and behaved in any of the social habits that I was accustomed to and expecting. He didn't shake hands with anybody or introduced himself to his students, his devotees and now he was inside the house. He certainly did not live up to the concepts and expectations I had already formed in my mind. Meanwhile, there's all these other people prostrated on the lawn and I don't feel any inclination to make a fool of myself by doing that. I thought: "People do pilgrimages and go to Jerusalem, the Holy Land, to walk in the same dust that Jesus might have walked in and here The Lord of the Universe just walked past me and took these steps by the front of the car and up the walk way and onto the porch and into the house. So I retraced his steps to the house and back to the car. Since everyone outside were focused on the young Guru in the house nobody paid any attention to me. Facing the driver's door of the Ferrari, I grabbed the door handle to pick up a vibe and nothing happened. I tried the door and it was unlocked so I opened the door and sat down in the driver's seat and shut the door. Like I said everybody was focused on the young Guru in the house and no one took notice of my behavior.

While I'm sitting in the driver's seat holding the steering wheel which was just touched by this "Lord of the Universe", I'm trying to pick up a vibe. I had also been told that this Guru was like a father to all of us so I decided to play the role of a young son in his father's car. This went on for maybe two or three minutes when I heard my mind say: "Boy are you in trouble.

ONE MAN'S SEARCH FOR THE DIVINE

If people find you in the car you're going to be chastised. You better get out of the car and hope that no one has seen you." So I got out of the car without anyone seeing me. People in front of the house were still focused on the Guru and yelling: 'Guru Maharaji, please come outside and be with us." This was all too bizarre for me and after a bit I walked back to the "premie house."

When I got back to the house there was a buzz of excitement with everyone. Chuck told me that Guru Maharaji would be speaking that evening in Boulder at Macky Auditorium at the University of Colorado. Chuck had befriended me, perhaps because we both grew up in New Hampshire, he in Hampton Beach and I in Manchester. He told me to get myself ready because I was going to ride with him. I got caught up in the energy of the anticipation that was resonating from everyone in the house. The opportunity of having "Darshan" which means being in the physical presence of the Guru was electrifying for all present except myself. I had never been around anyone that elicited that kind of excitement so I went along more as an observer than a participant after all I had seen the Guru that afternoon and I wasn't overwhelmed with a particular charge as I remember it was a bit anti-climactic.

We hurriedly had dinner of tofu, brown rice, and steamed vegetables and rushed off to Boulder. I road with Chuck and three others from the house. When we got to the event at Macky Auditorium the place was already three quarters full and we got seats about the twentieth row back and right in the middle. There was a short program of people singing songs that they had composed before the Guru came out. When the singing stopped the silence in the room was interrupted only by a few coughs and then a bit of a stir when this young boy who was now dressed in the traditional white Indian pajamas and in stocking feet walked out and everyone stood and cheered. He motioned for us to sit down and started speaking in English with a strong Indian accent. I had difficulty focusing on what he was saying because my mind had become very busy commenting on what he was saying or commenting on his English or the crowd around me. After about fifteen or twenty minutes I became very uncomfortable and wanted the whole thing to end. People in the audience were leaning forward in their seats listening to him and I observed how everyone seemed to be extremely focused and caught up on what he was saying.

Then I heard my mind say; "Look at these people. They're all mesmerized. He's got them in the palm of his hands and manipulating their minds. Hitler had similar power and look what happened to the Germans." Then came all the stories I had ever heard as a Catholic about the anti-Christ and Lucifer disguised as a saint. At that thought, I became extremely paranoid. I started to panic and became short of breath because I couldn't get out. There were people on both sides of me leaning forward and nobody was paying attention to me and I felt trapped. I didn't want to disturb anybody by trying to leave so I started to pray. Focusing on my heart, I prayed: "Please help me." I took a deep breath, instantly my paranoia went away. I relaxed and started focusing on what this teenage Guru was saying. My mind had shut up and I started feeling peaceful.

He told a story about a man who had given up looking for a Batman comic because he couldn't find one. And one day a young boy with a Batman comic in his back pocket approached the man and offered to give him a Batman comic but the man told the boy to leave him alone that, in fact, Batman comics don't exist. The boy replied that he had one in his back pocket and he could have it. Maharaji likened this story to that Master who travels the world offering the gift of peace and people tell him to "get real" that it doesn't exist and he shows them through the gift of Knowledge that peace is in fact real. I thought it was very wise to use a modern day parable to illustrate what he was offering.

I was moved and delighted by the program in Boulder and decided to cancel my plans to go to New Mexico and stay in Denver. The premies I was staying with invited me to stay and within a few days I shared a room with another guy. It also gave me a chance to see my daughter more often. Also, Krishna's charm had already rubbed off on everyone.

Some of the guys were working loading and unloading trailer trucks and invited me to join them. We would go to the truck terminal in the morning and get assigned a location then we would go and do the job. We would do two or three trailers a day and with sometimes four guys working it wouldn't take long to unload a trailer.

After about two weeks, my body was in pretty good shape. One day as we were loading a trailer I asked the driver where he was hauling to. He said that he was going to Minneapolis. I asked him if he would consider giving me a lift and I would help him unload his stuff on the way. He accepted and said that it wasn't a direct run. He would have to make deliveries to five different cities on the way. That was OK with me. I wasn't in any hurry. So my premie friends took me home to get my backpack and gear. They agreed to take care of Krishna while I was gone.

This was a new adventure for me. I had never ridden on a semicross-country before and again felt like a kid. At one of the stops, I called Elizabeth in Minneapolis and told her to expect to see me in a couple days. When we arrived in Minneapolis I went directly to Elizabeth's place of work and we drove back to her apartment and attempted to reconnect again. What I had not noticed was how much I had changed since I had received Knowledge. My values now were so different. Focusing on the relationship was no longer a priority for me. Playing house with someone and doing the furniture thing and the material thing had no appeal. There was even a lack of passion in our love making that was noticeable to both of us. After a couple of days, I decided to hitchhike back to Denver and Elizabeth drove me to the entrance of interstate 35 South and dropped me off not having made any plans to see each other again and we didn't.

The sign at the entrance ramp read: "Pedestrians, bicycles and mopeds prohibited beyond this point." So I stood at the entrance with my thumb out and after about an hour realized that there was no safe place for drivers to pull over and pick me up so I walked past the sign forbidding me to go any further and found a place on the ramp where a car could safely pull over and pick me up. I was willing to risk being arrested for disobeying the sign. I put my backpack down next to a folded $100 bill and of course I picked it up. I held it up to the sky and asked: "What's this for? Do you want me to fly instead? If I don't get a ride in the next hour I'll make arrangements to fly." About ten minutes later a man driving a new Mercedes Benz picked me up and asked me where I was going. I said that I was going to Sioux Falls, South Dakota. He said that he was going in that direction but would have to drop me off a hundred miles short of Sioux Falls. Fine with me. I'm not in any hurry. I was going there to visit Fred Fritchel, the Lutheran minister who had married me to my first wife in 1962. He had moved to Sioux Falls from Castlewood, South Dakota shortly after I got married and I wanted to tell him about my experience with receiving Knowledge and if he knew anything or had heard of anything like it.

The driver was well groomed and dressed in a three-piece suit. He was a wine salesman and a Vietnam veteran. We connected immediately. He told me that he was married and a father. If not for that he would probably be doing what I was doing: letting his beard and hair grow and getting stoned and hanging out. I mentioned that I had a dozen joints in my box of Marlboros and we could light one up. I didn't have to twist his arm so we got stoned while he was driving down highway 35 south and eventually connected to highway 90 west towards Sioux Falls. He shared his stories of Vietnam with me. Apparently he didn't see much combat. He and his fellow soldiers kept finding ways to get lost and get high on Vietnamese pot. I shared about my adventures of the past six months and at some point the driver volunteered to take me all the way to Sioux Falls.

When we pulled up in front of the minister's house, he reached underneath the front seat and pulled out a bottle of wine. "This is a very special bottle," he said. "Drink it at a special occasion and think of me." I took three joints out of my box of Marlboros and handed it to him and said: "Get high on these and think of me." We

88

parted ways without exchanging phone numbers. I often wonder if he still remembers picking up this hitchhiker and the short contact we had.

Fred and his wife graciously welcomed me to join them for dinner. During the dinner, I shared with them my journey and experience with this child Guru. I told them about my initiation into "the kingdom of God" and to my disappointment they were not impressed. I was invited to crash overnight in their basement. The following morning, breakfast was waiting for me when I got up and Fred drove me to the highway towards Denver. My good luck hitchhiking continued and the last ride I got took me to my door in Denver.

Some of the premies in the house were getting ready to fly to London to attend a Guru Puja festival with Maharaji. This is a festival specifically for the devotees to honor the living Perfect Master. Again for me it seemed a bit extreme to fly all the way to London and spend just a few days with this young boy I still had difficulty connecting with.

The only ones left in the house were Chuck Fellows whom I had befriended, Dick and his wife Jeffy and a teenager. Chuck, Dick, the teenager and I would work at loading and unloading semis and go home get stoned and have dinner. We all pretty much continued living the hippie drug induced lifestyle even though we all had received Knowledge. The only difference for me was that I was no longer suicidal, anxious, in pain and searching.

My practice of Knowledge was sporadic but fulfilling. I tried the best I could to relate to this teenage Guru, but it just wasn't working. I kept being told that the connection has to be from the heart, but that was too esoteric for me. My programming was so socially conditioned and Maharaji did not play that game. That summer I hung out with Chuck, Dick and Jeffy. We smoked a lot of pot together and continued taking hallucinogens.

My daughter Michelle spent a lot of time with me and got to know more about Maharaji and Knowledge. By the end of the summer, she had started getting herself prepared to receive Knowledge and before school started in September she received Knowledge. Nothing could have pleased me more because I knew that this practice would serve her for the rest of her life.

One July night around 1 AM we got a call from the trucking company that one of their semis had jackknifed as it was entering an exit ramp a little too fast and it turned over on its side. It was a freezer semi and we had to unload its cargo onto another semi. We were told that the cargo had been inspected and condemned. What

ONE MAN'S SEARCH FOR THE DIVINE

we found when we arrived at the site was a semi partly broken open with some of its cargo spilling out. There were boxes of all kinds of different cuts of frozen steak and boxes of frozen lobster tails and frozen king crab legs.

This truck was delivering to a steak house chain all over the west and had just started out. The load had been condemned by a government agency because they had discovered some crystallization on some of the steaks which meant the beginning of thawing and no longer frozen. So the load was condemned. Everyone involved with the unloading and destroying the cargo knew that it would never make it to the dump.

Part of the lifestyle at the premie house was a vegetarian diet. Although my fellow premies and I knew that some of this food was off limits to us it certainly wasn't off limits to our neighbors. So we started by loading up our van with boxes of steaks and lobster. There were also cheeses of all kinds, a different assortment of frozen pies, cheesecakes and cookies. There were also dozens of boxes of tootsie rolls. After filling up our van two of us stayed behind to continue the work and the third person rushed home with the cargo to be put into our large freezer at the ashram.

There was an unspoken understanding of what happened to the condemned load by our boss and everyone involved. That summer we made close friends with many of our neighbors. We distributed steaks and lobster to about a dozen houses. Kids were coming by on a daily basis to get tootsie rolls. We filled up the freezer of the owner of the local gas station. And we even exchanged some steaks for a rebuilt Volkswagen engine that we needed for our VW bus. In late August my mother, who lived in Orlando, Florida, called me to tell me about a dream that she had. She said: "Your father appeared to me last night all dressed in white with a beautiful smile. I told him about all my problems with the house and the property and my anxiety. He said: 'You have a son who's not busy. Call him up and ask him to come and help you.' So can you come and help me?" My father had been dead for two years and when he died, I was still married so it was bizarre that he knew I was available. I told my mother that I could be there in a couple of weeks and that I had a dog and I'd be hitchhiking. She was afraid for me and told me that she would send me some money to fly. So I made plans to visit her for a month. Up until then visiting my mother was not a very pleasant experience. Usually the first day of visiting her was nice.

The second day usually was about what I was doing wrong with my life and I'd be gone on the third day. Now that I had a way of getting in touch with inner peace, being with my mother would be a good test. About a week later I received a letter from her with fifty dollars to buy an airline ticket to fly from Denver to Orlando. Already I was being tested because no way was fifty dollars going to take care of my expenses for Krishna and myself. My lack of reaction to her small contribution to this

90

trip surprised me. I knew that it was a foreshadowing of things to come. And I came up with the rest of the money.

My oldest sister, Monique, who lived just down the block from my mother, picked me up at the airport and drove me and Krishna to my mother's house. It had been two and a half years since my father had died and my mother had been very dependent on him until the last few years of his life when leukemia and the experimental drugs eventually took its toll on his body. He had the task of taking care of the grounds and house repairs and since his death the place showed some neglect.

My mother had never been fond of animals so when she saw my dog her first response was to tell me that Krishna would have to sleep outside which I immediately vetoed. "Well okay then but if he pees or shits in the house, I'm not cleaning up after him," she said. My mother could gag at the mere mention of dog poop. I reassured her that we would keep things clean. Since mother was still working, my days were spent taking care of the property first by trimming the hedges and then doing what was necessary to bring the lawn back to life.

Three days after my arrival mother said: "I've been invited to a wedding in a couple of weeks and I want you to be my escort.""I'd love to. I like weddings." I said. "Good then. I'll take you to a hair dresser I know who'll give you a great haircut and then we'll go get you a suit, shirt and tie. Also, you're going to need new shoes to match. You certainly can't wear those trail boots with a suit.""Ma, I don't need any of that. I'll be fine just the way I am." "You can't go to a wedding dressed in jeans and boots and wear a ponytail and a beard." "Well, I'm not shaving or cutting off my pony tail and the clothes I have are just fine." "Then I'll go to the wedding alone. You're my son. I want you to look like someone I'm proud of not some hobo or homeless guy."

The following day as I was working in the yard, that familiar non-verbal voice got my attention. And basically the message was that I shouldn't be so resistant to my mother's requests nor be so attached to my external identity. As I contemplated assisting her to the wedding with a new physical look, my body started to relax. That night I greeted mother when she came home from work with the decision to go along with her to the wedding in my new look. She was so happy that I agreed to her request. I realized at that moment that I had spent a large part of my life defying her. It seemed that I had given her so much power that until now the only way that I dealt with it was to rebel. But in just the few moments that I spent allowing her to play in her own way, I grew up. There was a sense of openness and well-being with the lack of resistance that I was feeling.

The Saturday week before the wedding she took me shopping for clothes. I let her pick out the suit, shirt and matching tie. We got shoes and socks to match.

ONE MAN'S SEARCH FOR THE DIVINE

Then it was off to the hairdresser for a new hairstyle and a shave. Later I picked up a razor and shaving cream. The Saturday of the wedding was the first time since my separation that I mixed with straight people and I didn't have to pretend to be somebody I'm not. My mother was proud to introduce me as her son and I could allow her to be her and stayed centered and accepting of the whole event.

Many times as I was working in the yard I would have a revelation. One day as I was digging around in the yard I recalled a quote in the Bible by Jesus: "The Kingdom of heaven is within you." I had read or heard this Bible passage many times and it seemed that people: priests, nuns, ministers, always skipped over its meaning which had become deeply significant. It wasn't "the Kingdom of heaven is within you and you have to die first before you can experience it." I had never heard the ordained tell me that they would show me how to access that inner Kingdom. Not the priests. Not the nuns. Not the monks at St Anselm's college. Not the Ph. D. theologians at Augsburg college. Not even the pope that I recalled ever mentioned how to access the Kingdom of Heaven within. For me, that ignorance is criminal for any so-called spiritual leader. The only conclusion that I could come up with was that they had no idea what Jesus was talking about because they were void of the experience. I had received Knowledge about six months now and starting to feel that inner peace, that inner Kingdom on a daily basis. That "peace that passeth all understanding," was starting to make sense as an inner phenomenon.

It seemed that working with nature was conducive to many realizations that I had been having in the practice of Knowledge. On another day while I was working in the flower bed the passage in the bible that started to make sense was when Jesus talked to a Samaritan woman at the well and she offered him some water and he replied: "I will show you a well within you from which you will never thirst." I realized that I had been shown that well within me from which I could indulge myself to my hearts content.

Slowly the so-called mysteries were starting to make sense because I was experiencing them. It seemed so simple. The answers to the questions I had had as a child and told that the answers were mysteries to be discovered in Heaven were being revealed on a daily basis without ever asking the question. Another significant story from the Bible that I had heard many times was The Prodigal Son. I really think that the original title was The Prodigal Child. The story really applies to men as well as women. Anyway, according to the story this son goes to his father who is the king and asks his father for his inheritance. The son gets his money and goes away from his home and into society and parties until he blows through all his money. Once he's spent all he has, he no longer has any friends and finds himself destitute and longing.

92

In that state, he realizes how well off he had been in his father's estate and decides to go back humbled and to offer himself as just a mere servant in his father's estate. When he approaches his father's residence, the father sees him in the distance and runs to embrace him and welcome him home and celebrate his arrival. This is one of my favorite parables because one of the things I like about it is that the father doesn't go chasing after the son. He stays near the entrance of his own kingdom and waits for the son to come back and when he does there is rejoicing. It seems to me that we are all like the Prodigal Child. We leave the inner Kingdom because we have no clue of its preciousness and are catapulted into this world to become what our parents want us to be; what our culture wants us to be; what our society wants us to be; what our religion wants us to be. Because we don't know any better and neither do our caretakers, we abandon ourselves to please them so that we don't get killed and we split off from our true selves where we experienced what Harville Hendrix in his book Getting The Love You Want calls: "relaxed joyfulness." Have you ever looked at an infant and made eye contact? That infant will look at you without any embarrassment and without any impulse to be sociable. You might wave or say hello and they don't respond. Later on they're told by mom or dad to "be nice and say hello." My attitude is: just leave the kid alone and allow him to relate according to his own sense. By the time we are six or seven we are so socialized, so programmed that we have lost touch with our essence, our true self. Then we buy into society's promises about what will satisfy us or fulfill us or bring us happiness, or contentment. And it doesn't work. We even read in the great literatures of the world that "knowing ourselves" is the highest of all knowledges and we have no clue what that means nor do the Ph.Ds who teach it. When I focus on that beautiful, familiar and simple presence inside, I feel that peace. I feel that joy and to me it fulfills me and it is truly the Kingdom of Heaven within. It is truly returning to my inner father's Kingdom and I feel safe and at home. So it's amazing what a little work in nature in my mother's yard revealed to me.

I went to my mother's parish priest and with enthusiasm told him about my new revelations I was treated in a ho hum sort of way. When I approached the nuns at the local Catholic school with my new insights, they became a little skittish about what I was sharing because it wasn't something that the Church, as far as they knew, was promoting and they didn't want to be blasphemous so they humored me. After a while I gave up and felt very childish and quite naïve.

During this time, my cousin, Roger, who is twelve years younger than me was visiting his parents in Orlando. We had not seen each other for about ten years. Roger is an accomplished guitarist and had been following The Grateful Dead for many years. I introduced him to Shawn Philips and he introduced me to the Dead. It turned out that our musical interests were the same along with our taste for pot and psychedelics. We got together two to three days a week and would get stoned and often times would go and check out some bands. Roger was open to my discussions of Guru Maharaji and the Knowledge. So when the time came for me to leave Orlando and return to Denver, Roger followed me and started preparing himself to receive the Knowledge.

Once I got back to Denver, I realized that for me to truly root myself in the experience of Knowledge, I would have to be in an environment that was free of all temptations that fed my addictions. That environment was the Ashram, a monastic community. Ashram is a Sanskrit word meaning shelter or hermitage. Shelter was exactly what I needed. I let my intentions be known to whoever approved the candidates and before Thanksgiving of 1973 I was admitted into Guru Maharaji's Ashram.

There are certain rules one must live by as an Ashram resident. Illicit drugs, alcohol, tobacco and sex are not allowed. The diet is vegetarian and celibacy is also required and a discipline of meditation, service and Satsang must be practiced. So the schedule went like this: up at 6AM sing Aarti, a Hindu devotional song translated into English followed by a one hour practice in the techniques of Knowledge. Breakfast was followed with service until dinner time. Meals were to be eaten in silence and if someone got too chit chatty they were reminded to eat in silence. I learned to appreciate this ritual. I ate slower and was more in touch with my taste buds when I refrained from talking or listening to someone talk. I still prefer it to this day. After dinner, we attended Satsang from 7PM until 9PM. Satsang is also a Sanskrit word meaning a "spiritual discourse or sacred gathering." After Satsang, we again sang Aarti followed by the practice of Knowledge for an hour then bedtime. This daily ritual was practiced Monday through Saturday.

On Sunday, we practiced Knowledge in the morning for four hours followed by lunch. The afternoon was free to do what we wanted.

The first Ashram I was assigned to was with two married couples living celibately. Each couple had a one year-old child. There was a nineteen-year old girl and three single guys in their early twenties and myself. Each Ashram has a house mother and a house father. One of the married men, a recovering alcoholic was the house father who took care of the finances and the maintenance of the house. Any personal needs such as dental or medical went through the house father. Also, any disciplinary problems such as breaking the rules or not following the Ashram schedule were dealt by him. The nineteen year old girl was the house mother. She was the cook and in charge of the kitchen, buying groceries, laundry and coordinating with the house father for other personal needs like clothes, special diets, etc. The needs of each member were completely taken care of: shelter, food, medical, dental, clothing. Just as if we were living with a good parent. Even my child support was being paid. This care for Ashram residents was under the direction of Maharaji.

The first couple of weeks were like a honeymoon: everybody was glad to be there and we all got along. We all got up at six AM to sing Aarti followed by an hour of meditation. After breakfast, the men would leave for their jobs which supported the Ashram. In the evening, we would have dinner followed by two hours of Satsang and Aarti and one hour of practicing Knowledge. The honeymoon lasted no more than two weeks. Then people started having difficulty getting up at six, myself included. Rules were being violated. The mothers seemed to have privileges that the others didn't have because of the needs of their babies. Tension between the married couples was starting to show up. Did I mention that the women slept separately from the men? That's right. The married men slept with the single men in a dorm-like arrangement and the women slept in a separate room in the same kind of arrangement. Tension in the house was full blown within a month. The only relief was to stay focused inside and avoid getting caught up in someone else's trips. In the past, we could all deal with our discomfort with alcohol, drugs or sex. But now we have to deal with our discomfort by staying focused on service, Satsang, and meditation. And we were all novices. About six weeks after the opening, the nineteen-year old house-mother left with a nervous breakdown. The other women in the house were too occupied with their kids so I was asked if I would take over the duties of the house-mother which I accepted.

I had never cooked vegetarian before, so I followed some of the vegetarian cook books that we had. Tofu was relatively new to me so I had to learn many ways of preparing it so that the dinners wouldn't be too boring. Usually dinner consisted of brown rice, steamed vegetables and tofu. Breakfast was oatmeal or some dry cereal and fruit. Granola was a big deal. Pretty simple. I learned to grind my own wheat berries for making bread and baked about a dozen breads a week including banana nut bread with cinnamon. I made cinnamon rolls and croissants. This became a whole new education for me because I had a certain disdain for vegetarians since I had been a meat eater my whole life. Furthermore, my digestive system can't process legumes so I was constantly bloated with gas from the tofu. It sometimes made it difficult to meditate without farting every ten minutes.

I took my service as house-mother very seriously. There happened to be a book in the house on food combinations and after reading it I realized that, according to the book, some fruits I was making available for breakfast were incompatible with oatmeal so I eliminated the bananas. That morning the house-father asked me if there were any bananas in the house. When I answered that there were he asked me if he could have one.   And I said no because it was incompatible with what he had for breakfast. To his credit he didn't make a fuss about it and I felt so uncomfortable about denying him his banana that I put one in his lunch bag.

My service as house-mother extended perimeters that I didn't have before. I now had my own car to drive and a monthly budget to buy groceries, pampers, medicine if necessary, clothes and laundry. Whatever personal needs the Ashram residents had I took care of. There were about a dozen Ashram houses in Denver and about every two weeks the house-mothers would meet to meditate together, have Satsang, perhaps a snack and tea and talk about our problems and how to solve them.

One of the mothers in my house had the habit of leaving a dirty pamper right where she happened to change her baby. After having asked her many times to discard the pamper in a proper manner and having that request ignored, the next time I discovered a dirty pamper, I put it under her pillow and I never found another dirty pamper again and the subject was never brought up. I was learning communication skills that weren't in the books.

There seemed to always be a certain controlled tense feeling with a sprinkle of anxiety in the Ashram. The regulated schedule and the lack of substances to alleviate any discomfort took its toll. One day while I was trying to comfort one of the crying babies and the house-father was trying to comfort his own child, we got into an intense argument over something trivial and if we hadn't been holding these babies I have no doubt that we would have come to blows. As we were staring at each other in a state of rage we just happened to connect eyeball to eyeball and the whole drama went away like a puff of smoke and we both experienced an overwhelming inner peace. As we shared the experience, we realized that there was a grace present that transcended our difficulties.

Much more effective than alcohol or pot.

We had all been in this particular house for about three months and all starting to become a bit more comfortable with the routine when it was announced that Maharaji would be giving Darshan the next day, Valentine's day. I had heard about this ritual by other devotees and how wonderful it was, but I had never experienced it myself. What I was told was that you go before the Master and kiss his feet and he gives you his personal blessings. The first time a devotee has Darshan, he can ask for Holy Breath by cupping his hand behind his right ear and the Master blows one of his breaths to the devotee. The kissing of the feet I was familiar with in a different way.

96

As a Catholic, we used to go to church on Good Friday for services and kneel down at the communion rail while thepriest went by with a crucifix and we would kiss the feet of the crucifix. So kissing the feet of the Master was not so strange except that this master was a living entity. So I was looking forward to the experience with much curiosity. I knew that my daughter, Michelle, was going to be off on Valentine's Day, so I asked her mother to let her spend the day with me and she agreed.

The next day, Valentine's Day, it seemed that everyone in the house was very irritable including myself. I drove to Michelle's house and picked her up. She had brought some dress up clothes with her and on the way back to the Ashram I went to the local market and got a flower for everyone to bring to Darshan. We all got into our Sunday best and drove to the office building in downtown Denver where the national headquarters were.

The hall where all this was to happen was still being set up so we had to line up in the stairwell leading up to the third floor. We waited about two hours as they were preparing the hall and in the meantime many of us were getting more and more tense and impatient.

Again I went into this whole inner dialogue about how disrespectful it was to make us wait this long and how inconsiderate and becoming more and more judgmental and critical about how things were being organized. The tension in the staircase seemed to have reached a crescendo when a baritone voice started singing Amazing Grace. Within seconds, everyone joined in and it broke the intense spell of dissatisfaction. When the song was finished, the door to the hall opened and we all streamed in quietly and reverently.

Maharaji was sitting on a chair on an elevated platform so that we barely had to bend over when we kissed his feet. People started lining up to start the procession to the Master's feet and Michelle was in front of me. As we got closer and closer to Maharaji, it seemed like everything went into slow motion. I saw her kiss his feet and ask for Holy Breath and walk away. Then I bent over to kiss his feet. He was wearing blue silk socks with some lipstick marks on them. As I kissed his feet I heard my mind say: "Blue socks?" Then I stood up and cupped my hand behind my right ear to receive Holy Breath as Maharaji was talking to someone standing to his right. I don't know how many seconds went by before he acknowledged me but when he saw me he put his hand by his mouth and it appeared like he threw a breath at me then he went back talking to the person on his right. I didn't realize until that moment how numb I had been because I didn't feel a thing and I again heard my mind say: "Big deal." I continued following the procession past Maharaji with Michelle in front of me still in a slow motion state of awareness. It looked like she was going to pass out and somebody helped her to a chair. I had taken maybe three or four steps by then when I finally took a breath and it seemed that that breath came from a place deep inside of me that seemed infinite and as it rose up my body and expanded into my heart area, I felt a sense of love that was so profound and intense that my knees buckled and somebody helped me over to a chair. Every breath I took after that was the same feeling. Overwhelmed with joy, I cried like a baby. The tears came without resistance. I know that if I had held back the tears I would have exploded, the feeling was so intense. I knew then that this was the love I had always wanted to feel but often doubted that it was possible. I wasn't crazy or idealistic after all. What I was looking for truly exists. This intense feeling of love with every breath lasted about three hours until I guess I started getting used to it. Later on when I expressed to Maharaji about the love that I felt and told him how loving he was he asked: "Where do you feel that love?" I pointed to my chest and said: "Here in my heart."

"What do you think that is?"

"It's your love."

"No, it's your love that you feel. That is you. I'm here to reveal it to you. I'm just a mirror."

Another time when I sensed a deep kindness in Maharaji's exchange with a man in a difficult place. I remembered what he had said previously about feeling love, so I played out a similar scene in my mind that went something like this: "You are so kind."

He replied: "Where do you feel that kindness?"

I pointed to my chest and he said: "That's your kindness that you feel. I can't give you that feeling. You already have it within you. I'm just a mirror to help you feel it."

It took me years to accept that this incredible treasure was within me because my mind was always so quick at showing me what a shit I was and all the bad things I had done in my life. It is still good at reminding me about all the people I hurt and all the stupid decisions that I've made but when I tune into my heart none of those judgments exist. I can drink from that well of love until I'm totally fulfilled, until my "cup runneth over."

About two weeks after Darshan our house was disbanded and the residents were placed in other houses and I was placed in a house with just men to be their housemother. The state of affairs in the new house was a lot lighter and more spacious. I had my own room. I also learned about new culinary needs with some of the residents. There were two men, we called each other "brother", who were not only vegetarians but were also dairy free or as they called it "mucus free". I had to learn to cook for their special needs. At first I had a lot of resistance to these unique needs. I had been conditioned at home to eat what was in front of me. The idea that someone could ask and receive a meal different than what others at the table were getting I judged as self-indulgent. When I mentioned my reaction to the house-father, he replied that it wasn't my business to determine someone else's needs and that my duty was to serve. So I had to stretch that intention of service and felt freed up from some of my conditioning.

During this time, I was also interested in becoming part of the Unity School Ashram in Denver. In 1972 Maharaji had asked some former teachers to start a school so that the children of Premies could have an alternative to the public school system. When asked what philosophy of education the new school should follow, the response was: "I never went past the sixth grade. What do I know about education? You guys are the educators.

You figure it out." I can imagine a bunch of teachers coming together to decide on a philosophical approach to education could be a problem. Each teacher in essence has his or her unique philosophy so how to come up with an approach that everyone would agree upon could be a problem. Then someone mentioned Waldorf, the system of education that Rudolf Steiner created in 1919. With the combined educational training that these teachers had, no one had ever heard of Waldorf. So much for our educational systems.

Anyway after looking into Steiner's system of education, everyone agreed to align their teaching methods according to a radically new focus. Not that Waldorf is radical but compared to the American public school system it is radical. The following is from an article Why Waldorf Works: "For the Waldorf student, music, dance, and theater, writing, literature, legends and myths are not simply subjects to be read about, ingested and tested. They are experienced. Through these experiences, Waldorf students cultivate a lifelong love of learning as well as the intellectual, emotional, physical and spiritual capacities to be individuals certain of their paths and to be of service to the world."

When I first expressed my desire to join the teacher's Ashram, I talked to Sharon, the director of the school. She told me that I must show my interest by coming to the school as often as possible to do service in whatever capacity was needed. So again and again when I had free time I would drive to the school and contributed my services as it was needed. Sometimes it would be to weed the garden or help in the kitchen. Other times it may be to help with laundry or drive the kids home after

ONE MAN'S SEARCH FOR THE DIVINE

school or even pick them up in the morning. I was also invited to attend some of the lectures by Waldorf trainers and encouraged to read some of Steiner's works.

At some point, in late Spring of 1974, arrangements were made for me to transfer to the Unity School Ashram. I was asked to take a job to financially support the Ashram so I got a job driving a truck for the Rocky Mountain News delivering adds to the subscribers.

After about two months, the cook asked to be relieved so I was asked to replace her which I accepted. I now had to fix, with some help, breakfast, lunch and dinner for about thirty people a bit of a stretch from cooking for seven or eight people. I had two stoves to work with; a large preparation area; large containers of honey, brown rice, flour and other staples. My budget for food was $2.40 a day per person which didn't seem like much to me, but I always had enough money to do special meals at the end of the month. I bought the food in bulk: butter, cheeses, milk, brown rice, millet, tofu, etc. I often enjoyed preparing bread and pastries the night before and bake them for breakfast. People seemed satisfied with my food and I often received rave reviews for my culinary art. Cooking always seemed natural for me and managing a kitchen was second nature. When the last Sunday of the month came, I always made a special four course banquet with special linens and candles. Stuffed mushrooms followed by a salad and tofu Stroganoff with a strawberry/rhubarb cream pie for dessert could be a typical end of the month dinner.

Sometimes there were complaints that the meals did not comply with a life of austerity but I never saw in the rule book that enjoying gourmet foods were forbidden. During this time at Unity School, I also attended training classes to become a Waldorf teacher.

Every few months Maharaji would call a gathering of the Ashram residents to encourage us to keep practicing the Ashram discipline. Once he must have seen that many of us were experiencing confusion and he said: "If you're experiencing confusion, that's good, because it means that you're doing the practice. It's like that deep sea diver when he hits the floor of the ocean, he kicks up a lot of dirt. He just has to wait until the cloud of dirt settles down and then he can see clearly again. And that is what is happening with you. You've gone so deep that it kicked up all this garbage and if you keep practicing Knowledge eventually clarity happens." These messages always gave me a sense of relief because although I was diligent in my practice I often had difficulty with my mind. There was a part of me that wanted out of there every day. My addictions were not being met and it seemed that my legs were always in the process of running away to get high or drink or get laid or all three. But one morning after about six months in the Ashram I realized I no longer had the anxiety

100

to leave and a sense of inner peace and calmness had taken over. I was so relieved.

Just because we live a spiritual practice it doesn't mean that addictive impulses totally vanish. One day I happen to be riding my bike around the neighborhood when I rode past a triple X theatre and the old addictive impulse with pornography surfaced. The feeling is hard to describe. It's a bit like adrenaline but and every bit as addictive. I had not felt that drug for a couple of years yet there it was flowing through my veins again. I was a bit confused, but I quickly pedaled back to the Ashram. For the next couple of days, the impulse to go see a pornographic movie kept surfacing and it was noticeably strong during meditation. I was so ashamed that I just kept it to myself. Within a couple of days I watched myself ride my bike to the XXX theatre, buy a ticket and watch for about a half hour a very violent pornographic movie from South America. I was so overwhelmed with disgust, adrenaline, and whatever chemicals are released from the brain that I left. As I rode my bike back the feelings of shame preyed on my mind like a dense dark, heavy fog.

I was in an altered state of mind and I couldn't shake it. I felt dirty, and unworthy to be in Maharaji's Ashram and felt too disgusted with myself to talk to anyone. I felt totally alienated from everyone. That night during the practice of Knowledge, my mind once again attacked me by telling me what a scum bag I was and that I was flawed to the core without any chance for redemption. I started having thoughts of suicide. Notwithstanding all these distractions, I continued to practice and beg for mercy. Sleep that night was very active and without much relief. The following morning I sang Aarti with everyone and then went into the practice but this time with less mental activity.

After breakfast, I went and took a shower and stood under the sprinkling water and imagined the darkness being washed away. A little while later as I was moving the shaver through the shaving cream, I happen to focus on the eyes of the person in the mirror looking at me and I became overwhelmed with such love. I know it sounds weird. It was me looking at me from the mirror but not through the veil of my mind but from the unconditional love in my heart. The feeling of love was so powerful that it washed away all the shame that I had been feeling and quiet tears of joy slowly made a path through the shaving cream on my face. I was jubilant, finished shaving and went to the kitchen to start lunch preparations. I have shared this experience with very few people.

That summer Maharaji had a three day program on the University of Massachusetts campus in Amherst, Massachusetts. I was given the service to drive some of the kids and their mothers to the program. Since we didn't have much for funds we switched drivers and drove until we arrived in Amherst nineteen hundred miles and

ONE MAN'S SEARCH FOR THE DIVINE

thirty hours later.

These programs are always pleasurable and to some extent stressful and anxiety provoking. The feeling of being with the living Master of the time and receiving his blessings are difficult to describe. Suffice it to say that it is always worth the effort energetically and financially.

One of the delightful surprises at the event was seeing my uncle Rolland, Roger's father. He had received Knowledge earlier in the year and had never seen Maharaji in person. When the opportunity for receiving Darshan was made available we stood side by side along some of the roads on campus and Maharaji sat on a specially rigged chair on the side of a jeep and was driven very slowly by us so that we would have a chance to kiss his feet and those who had not received Holy Breath could also ask by cupping their hand behind the ear. Rolland happen to be standing next to me when Maharaji went by.

For a long time afterwards Rolland stood still and had this great smile with tears running down his face. I could tell that his heart had been deeply touched even without him saying a word. I still remember that look on his face.

Soon after returning to Denver, Sharon, the school director, told me that in preparation for teaching I would have to go to Milwaukee, Wisconsin for a ten day training at the Waldorf training center. Another teacher, Michael Blakemore, and I were to hitchhike to Milwaukee because there was not enough money for air-fare. Fortunately I could rely on my past experiences on the road to make this trip with Michael. That Sunday we were driven to the highway 76 and began hitchhiking with our backpacks. It was a warm sunny day and we were nonchalant about the whole thing walking along side the road with our thumbs out. Within about an hour somebody stopped and asked us if we would be interested in driving some rental trucks to Des Moines, Iowa because the trucks were needed there and we would be paid 25 dollars each. We jumped right on that opportunity.

The driver took us to the location of the rental agency where other drivers were waiting and Michael and I jumped into our trucks and joined the caravan of trucks towards highway 80 and on to Des Moines. I'm always amazed at the magic of it all.

When we left Des Moines 25 dollars richer, it seemed to us that we would have a better chance getting a ride if we split up so I headed out before Michael and got a ride to Chicago. It was dark when I arrived and wondered if I was going to spend the night on the road or in Milwaukee when as luck would have it someone picked me up who was going to Milwaukee. When I arrived I called the Ashram and they sent a driver to pick me up. I might have arrived earlier if I had driven myself but making it in one day hitchhiking was quite impressive. Michael arrived the next day after having to spend the previous night in a cheap hotel.

The Waldorf training started on Monday with a lesson in eurythmy an expressive movement art originated by Rudolph Steiner. The gestures one expresses relate to the sounds and rhythms of speech, to the tones and rhythms of music and to soul experiences, such as joy and sorrow. It is mostly unstructured and I was very self-conscious in trying to express with body movement without a little direction. Because of the positive reinforcement of the teacher I was able to let go of my inhibitions enough to feel and express. What I really needed was to smoke a joint then I could make a fool of myself and not worry about it.

Water colors were another class that forced me to let go of inhibitions and self criticism. Steiner saw different pigments as having certain soul qualities and one could see the uniqueness of each pigment by having a wet watercolor paper on a slant board and applying different pigments to the paper and observing how each one expresses.

After a few hours of this, I could see what Steiner was seeing. It was like a foreign language in color form. Later on before the dinner break the class went to the local park to do a "community painting." There was a large water color paper on the ground and each of us would have three minutes to paint whatever we wanted on this paper. When the last person was finished we could choose to embellish what we had done. At the end of the class the teacher held up the paper and said: "Look at all these egos. There's an ego there and there and there. This is not a community painting. These are all isolated and individual expressions." He said nothing after that and we went home. The next day in the community painting class the first person who painted covered the full paper. While this is going on I was thinking; "Man he's taking up all the room, how narcissistic."

Then the next person went up and covered the previous persons work and I thought: "Oh shit the first guy is going to be pissed," but he wasn't. Then I got what was going on. By the time my turn came I added my two cents worth and when we were all finished no one could tell who had done what. Our teacher was pleased. With very little direction we started to understand about community.

The section on fairy tales and mythology was one of my favorites In Waldorf, the teacher doesn't read the stories. He first learns the story, integrates the meaning and then relates the story to the children being very careful not to influence by tone of

ONE MAN'S SEARCH FOR THE DIVINE

voice or gestures. The next day the children would retell the story and possibly sketch it out. These lessons reminded me of my godmother when she would visit us and read us fairy tales.

After ten days of fairy tales, watercolor classes, eurythmy and lectures it was time to return to Denver. I had decided to take a detour and return via Minneapolis to see Richard Sargent, a former English teacher at Augsburg College. Richard was interested in what I had been doing since I left school and especially the training in Waldorf since he now had a young son. I shared with him and his wife what I had learned and after an overnight they drove me to route 35 to begin hitchhiking. I was standing with my thumb out by one of the bus stations on the freeway when a police cruiser pulled up and arrested me for breaking the law. I was taken downtown and put in the city jail until my arraignment.

Being in jail for the first time in my life was a bit surreal even more so because of the other prisoners. There was a guy wearing a three piece suit arrested for non-payment of traffic violations. There were four tall black guys waiting arraignment for bank robbery.

The story they told me was that they were University of Wisconsin students and also on the basketball team. Earlier in the week while they were sharing a joint they started fantasizing about robbing a bank so they drove to Minneapolis and got caught robbing a bank. After a lunch of American cheese sandwiches on dry white bread we were arraigned. When my name came up and the charges were read, the female judge became very upset with the police officers for wasting the courts time with what she considered a minor infraction. She dismissed the case and told the arresting officers to drive me to the highway going West where it would be safe for me to hitchhike. I did my best to avoid smirking as they were driving me to the designated spot. I thanked them for their service when they dropped me off. A few minutes later I had a ride.

When we got back to Denver, I was told by Sharon that I would be teaching two French classes: a first grade French class and a seventh grade French class. This became a major challenge for me because I had never taught a regular class, let alone a French course. I had done only substitute teaching in the past and felt totally inadequate. I felt totally confronted with my lack of skills. I felt totally inept at preparing for classes. For the first graders, I was to conduct the class completely in French.

The fairy tales were to be told in French with no translation. I had a lot of doubts about these methods, but I remembered that when I first came to the U. S. at the age of seven I had been put into a school that was totally submerged in English and I pretty much understood everything that was said. So it was no different for these kids to be taught only in French. I researched French songs for kids that they could learn and on Fridays we would set up the room like a café. The kids would play roles like a maitre d', patrons and waiters and waitresses. Lemonade or grape juice would simulate white and red wine and there were always hors d'oeuvres and little sandwiches served followed by perhaps chocolate mouse or some kind of dessert. At times, the French baguette was served along with some cheeses. I had taught them some of the French drinking songs from my own childhood such as Chevaliers de la Table Ronde (Knights of the Round Table) and Plantons la Vigne (Planting the Vines). We would all stand up and sing and swing our "wine" glasses and the kids, needless to say, always looked forward to Fridays.

The seventh grade was a little more difficult. There were five girls in the class ranging in age from twelve to thirteen and they always seemed bored. Learning a foreign language was the last thing on their mind and I was totally inept regarding discipline and even more inept in teaching the subject and you can only fake for so long when eventually it became very noticeable that I didn't know what I was doing but too embarrassed to seek help. I did teach them one song that they enjoyed and that was the French love song from South Pacific: Dites Moi.

The fall of 1974 I struggled with preparation for my French classes even though I didn't know what I was doing most of the time. Learning the Waldorf methods of education from a conceptual level was a total mystery for me and I didn't confide in anyone about the perpetual self doubt and anxiety that I was having. I also had terrible discipline problems with the teenage seventh grade girls. Sometimes I would resort to using a pressure point tactic on the arm to enforce discipline but that backfired when one of the students developed a black and blue mark on her arm. There was a lot of criticism from the parents about my discipline methods. Other teachers also expressed their concerns about my methods. I finally resigned myself to letting the chaos happen and started losing interest in teaching. Perhaps teaching in this kind of setting just wasn't for me.

One benefaction of my position at the school happened on the day that Maharaji visited the school. The day prior we were given advanced notice to prepare for his coming. He would be coming to my class in the afternoon when I would be with the seventh grade girls. We rehearsed the song from South Pacific and changed the word from "Mademoiselle" to Maharaji. The song goes like this:

Dites-moi pourquoi la vie est belle?

Dites-moi pourquoi la vie est gaie?

ONE MAN'S SEARCH FOR THE DIVINE

Dites-moi pourquoi cher Maharaji?

Est-ce-que parce-que vous m'aimez?

The translation goes something like this:

Tell me why life is so beautiful?

Tell me why life is so joyful?

Tell me why dear Maharaji?

Is it because you love me?

When the day arrived for Maharaji's visit there was much excitedment in the air. He first went to visit the first graders on the first floor then he walked up to the second floor classroom and walked in with his wife, Marolyn, and a few others. It seemed that when he walked in, the room expanded into twice the size. He looked around and I wanted him to stay as long as possible so I said: "Maharaji can we sing you a song"? In his kind way, he said: "Yes." When he said: "Yes" it was like the whole Universe was saying "yes." It wasn't just "yes you can sing me a song" but "yes" to everything. So I turned towards the girls and directed them to sing: "Dites-moi" then I turned to Maharaji standing just two feet away from me, looked into his eyes and continued singing. I don't know whathappened to me, but I think I left my body or went into some Divine state. What I experienced defies explanations. In any case, I blew the song and as I did I must have come back from wherever I went and people were laughing. A minute or two later

Maharaji and his entourage left and I was in a state of bliss that I had never experienced before. It is said in some of the literature about the relationship between the devotee and the Guru that the Guru is like a tuning fork resonating at a very high frequency and when the devotee surrenders and allows himself to be finely tuned, he starts to resonate according to his Divine nature. Many times I had heard Maharaji tell us: "I don't want to take away your guitar. I just want you to tune it up." I guess I was being finally tuned.

That night there was a community program with the possibility that Maharaji might attend and when he didn't show up I wasn't disapppointed because I was still resonating from the bliss. This high, as I call it lasted for three days. I hardly slept and everything I did seemed to be effortless. I was happy, joyful, easy to get along with and it seemed thatmy feet barely touched the ground. On the third day, I walked to the library about a mile away to get some French song books for children. Walking

106

back to the school, still in a state of bliss, I had to walk across an overpass and half way across I heard my mind say: "Jump off the bridge." It was not only a voice but an inner impulse. It scared the hell out of me and I ran across the overpass and tried to figure out what the hell had just happened. My body was filled with extreme distress. The bliss was gone and now I was in a state of immense confusion and pain. My recourse was to practice one of the Knowledge techniques that we called Holy Name and anchor myself there. Whenever I forgot to practice I would be back in hell. I had to choose between experiencing heaven or hell moment to moment. A few days after the overpass incident I spoke to Ron Coletta about my experience. Ron was often with Maharaji at his house and he understood what I had gone through. He told me that he often had a similar experience of distress when Maharaji went away and that he too had to be diligent in his practice. That conversation with him gave me some relief and I also realized that I wasn't insane.

Andre Patenaude

PART II

FALLING OUT OF GRACE

When Christmas vacation was approaching, I called my sister, Huguette, in Beverly Hills, California and asked her if she would like to have her brother visit her for the holidays. She was excited about the posibility of my visit, so I asked permission from the school director to leave the school for ten days. She told me that the school had no money for me to make the trip but if I could get some money from the local headquarters it would be okay. Intuitively I was wishing that money would not be available so I would not be able to go but I had been granted twenty five dollars for the trip and a ride was arranged with some premies who were driving to the Los Angeles area and needed another person to share gas expenses.

When my ride arrived at the school to pick me up on Sunday December 22nd, I almost canceled. It was a rusty 1956 Chrysler 4-door sedan with one rear shock that didn't seem to be working right because it looked like the car was tilting in such a way that it appeared to be riding sideways. I figured that I had been pretty adventurous so far and backing down at the last minute didn't seem fair so I jumped in with my small suitcase and we took off with enthusiasm and optimism. The driver was the mother of one of my first grade students who was also one of the passengers and there was a woman of about twenty five that I had seen volunteer at the school and myself. We had a little over a thousand miles to go and with alternating drivers we figured to be arriving in Beverly Hills about early afternoon the following day.

The lead driver knew Beverly Hills well so when we arrived in the Los Angeles area, we headed in the direction of Tower road where my sister lived. After asking for directions from a UPS driver, we found the address and I was dropped off. There was nobody home so I sat on a bench in the driveway. After about an hour, I wondered if I was at the right house. Then I started looking through the windows to see if I could recognize something that was associated with my sister but everything seemed strange.

After double checking the address I started checking doors in case one of them was unlocked. I eventually found a screen door in the back of the house that led to the swimming pool and let myself in. About an hour later my sister, Huguette and her daughter, Kim, arrived in her blue TR6 and she was quite surprised to see me. We got reacquainted and a little while later her husband, Don, arrived. Don was an

109

ONE MAN'S SEARCH FOR THE DIVINE

African American about ten years older then my sister about six feet tall and built like a boxer. He was quite impressed by the fact that I had let myself in when no one was there. Some pleasantries were exchanged and a few minutes later both Huguette and Don excused themselves and went into their bedroom and shut the door. A few minutes later Huguette emerged and she showed me the back bedroom where I would be sleeping. I unpacked and she helped me put on clean sheets on the bed then we went back into the living roomand I said: "Do you still smoke pot?"

"Yeah. I just had a couple of hits with Don when I went into my bedroom. I didn't want to smoke in front of you since you told me that you were a monastic."

"Do you mind sharing some of it with me?" I asked.

She laughed and said: "I thought that you were really straight and no I don't mind sharing my pot with you and by the way it's really good Columbian." So she brought out her pot and rolled a joint and we smoked it together. This was the first pot I had smoked in over a year. Soon a girlfriend of hers named Felicia arrived, a beautiful, tall, Hispanic woman with a gleaming smile. She joined us for some pot and before long I became very attracted to her. I volunteered to give her a foot massage and she promptly took off her shoes. In the process, I offered her a full body massage then we went into my bedroom, she took off her clothes and we had sex instead. During all this time, I justified breaking my Ashram vows by telling myself that I wasn't in the Ashram. I was now back into my old addictive ways of thinking and behaviors and relishing in it.

The day before Christmas my sister announced that we would be having roast turkey for Christmas eve dinner. I told her that I was a vegetarian now and when her husband heard that he said: "You'll have to eat what the rest of the family eats." So that night I had animal protein for the first time in almost two years. As I ate, a voice in my head told me that I would get sick from eating turkey and the power of suggestion did its trick and I got a stomach ache. Christmas night, prime rib was served and as I bit into the meat the same annoying voice in my head told me that I was going to get sick again from eating this meat. This time I cancelled that thought and told myself that I would be OK and I was. Boy did I get a good dose of the power of suggestion.

The rest of the week was just more partying. Felicia became my companion when she was not working and we indulged in getting high and enjoying each others bodies. I made up for eighteen months of celibacy in one week. Huguette also had a friend, Fran, whohad been a Las Vegas showgirl and was now a coke dealer. Fran was at the house often and I got to experience my first snort of coke. It was the strangest experience for me, the back of my throat swelled up and it made me gag and I couldn't for the life of me understand the attraction to this drug let alone the addiction. Pot was more my drug of choice.

During this time, I was also doing some hands on healing with whoever came to the house that was hurting. For some reason, my hands were emitting powerful healing energies that I had not been aware of. It started when my sister had a headache and I did a bit of work around her neck and head. Then when someone would show up and be hurting or not feeling good, Don, her husband would say: "Go see André and have him put his hands where you're hurting." And I would. It seemed like a bit of a game to me, but it was working so I went along with it. Don would say to me something like: " You're wasting your talents in this monastic life your leading. You should be doing healings and I can get you all the patients to keep you busy." Just enough of those comments seeped through into my ego that I gave it some consideration which, as you'll see became my fall from grace.

New Years Eve came around and a big party had been planned in the house. Huguette got me some new clothes to wear since she didn't find my Ashram attire very attractive.

That night I had new pants and shirt unbuttoned halfway down my chest. I was given a medallion to wear. Again I had decided earlier that week to just go with his ride that I was on. No resistance. Guests started to arrive around nine o'clock. The women were all gorgeous and dressed seductively with plenty of cleavage. There was a great party atmosphere as the hors d'oeuvres were passed around and the champagne flowed. There were trays of previously rolled joints everywhere and mirrors with mounds of coke moving from guest to guest. I guess, because of my lack of experience with coke, I wasn't allowed to hold the mirrors for fear that I would spill some or drop it so it was usually the women who would scoop out some of the white powder with their little silver spoons and hold it up to my nose and tell me to snort it. After a few hits, I had to stop them because I just didn't like the effect. I noticed that Felicia didn't snort either.

Eventually, I got bored with the whole evening and faked illness and went to bed. This was not a lifestyle that I could keep up with.

The following day my ride back to Denver showed up about noon and before I left, Don, my brother-in-law reminded me of his offer to promote me and my healing hands and also gave me some uppers for the drive as he bid me farewell. When we got to Palm Springs, I took over the driving and all I could think about was the week that had passed: the drugs, the women, the hands on healing, the possibility of setting up an office to do healings. My ego really got into it and I could imagine people lining

ONE MAN'S SEARCH FOR THE DIVINE

up to see me and I would become famous and make a lot of money. With the speed I had taken my mind was running a hundred miles an hour and I started to seriously consider moving to Beverly Hills sometime in the future.

About eighty miles from Denver on route 25 around 3 AM I was stopped by a state trooper for a burned out tail light. He told me to turn off the engine and after checking my license and the car registration he gave us a ticket. We got back in the car while he was till parked behind us and the car wouldn't start because the battery was dead. We had jumper cables, but the trooper would not let us connect the cables to his car and made up some story about it being against policy. So much for their slogan about being public servants. We asked him to call AAA and he also refused. He drove off and left us stranded. At that time of the morning there wasn't much traffic so it took a couple of hours before somebody finally stopped to give us a battery boost so that we could get home.

Back to my other life in the Ashram now seemed different. It felt like a part of me had been left behind in California and my dedication to my service as a Waldorf teacher and maintaining my vows were diminished considerably. My performance as a teacher became less and less acceptable and by April it was decided by the school administrator and some of the staff that I should resign. It came as no surprise to me and in a way I was relieved because I had a hard time implementing the Waldorf concepts. It was suggested that I get together with Rennie Davis who was working on some kind of community service. That was appealing to me. I liked Rennie and we got along pretty well but before I pursued that service I called my sister Huguette in Beverly Hills and investigated further the offer of setting up a healing clinic for me that her husband Don had proposed when I was visiting during the holidays. Sure enough, they told me to come out to California and we could get started.

When I told Sharon, the school director, about my plans she was skeptical about my intentions. She said: "André I've observed how pure you have gotten in your disciplined practice of meditation, service and satsang and that the lure of the world could distract you from the purity you have found within your heart and I'm concerned that you could lose all the depth that you've so fervently worked for. I give you my blessings no matter what your decision is." I knew what she was talking about because as far as I was concerned I had already lost that purity during my holiday visit. It seemed that my spiraling out of grace had already happened and I was mostly in denial.

I had heard my teacher, Maharaji, talk about how powerful the mind is and how seductive it can be. He would often say to not fight with my mind because I would lose or join it because again I would lose. Just ignore it and let it do its thing, he

Andre Patenaude

would say. I suppose I still had an opportunity to redeem myself, but my ego had been stroked by the folks in Beverly Hills to such an extent that I was completely helpless.

Within two weeks after my dismissal at the school Ashram my one-way airline ticket from Denver to Los Angeles which Huguette had sent me arrived and I had a friend drive me to the airport. I was to have a big lesson between living in the fantasy world of my sister and her husband and my inner very practical life I had been discovering as a monastic for the last eighteen months.

Huguette picked me up at LAX in her TR6 convertible and before we left the airport property I was given a joint to light up. It's funny how spiraling downward seems so euphoric. It is said that it's not the fall that kills you, it's the sudden stop at the bottom.

That bottom would come soon enough. We drove to the house on Tower Road and since they didn't have a live in maid I got settled in the maid's quarters. I had my own personal entrance, bathroom with shower and close to the kitchen. That night there was a small celebratory dinner on my behalf and was told that arrangements for my clinic were not finalized and would I mind assisting at their office until the clinic is ready.

My sister and Don had opened up a cosmetic surgery referral office and also did pregnancy testing and referred pregnant women who wanted an abortion to an abortion clinic. I agreed to help out and they would give me $500 a month for my services. I learned how to pitch face lift procedures over the phone and when potential clients came in I could show them before and after pictures for just about any cosmetic surgery procedures. In one of the drawers of my desk I had a breast implant silicone bag. I often would play with it and try to imagine fondling a breast and feeling the silicone. Somehow it just didn't feel natural. Sure it looks good once the implant is in and the scars no longer appear but implants never look natural to me. When a woman would come in to inquire about breast augmentation (a preferred term to "breast implants") I would reach into the drawer and throw the silicone bag on the desk and say: "This is what they're going to put into your chest." Then I would show them before and after pictures, quote the price and regardless of all my attempts to discourage them from having the procedure done they often would undergo the procedure.

The pregnancy testing was a little tricky. Sometimes the readings would be very obvious one way or the other and sometimes the readings weren't clear. When that was the case I would have them make an appointment with the doctor who did the abortion and he would test again. On occasion a mother would bring in her thirteen or fourteen year old daughter for pregnancy testing with the insistence on abor-

113

ONE MAN'S SEARCH FOR THE DIVINE

tion if the test was positive. I maintained a neutral point of view with the abortion thing. My business was to do the testing and then let the patient make the decision.

One month went by and then another and still no healing clinic. The story line was always: "we're looking for the best possible location for you." I always went along with the program. I guess there was a part of me that didn't feel totally trusting of my gifts as a healer especially now that my discipline of meditation and service had diminished considerably. Oh I did meditate but not with the regularity and consistency and focus that I had in the Ashram. I practiced meditation just enough to maintain. There was Satsang going on every night in a hall above the Baskin/Robbins ice cream parlor on Larchmont Drive and I attended quite often just to keep in touch with the local community. The practice of Knowledge or the meditation is about experiencing oneself. At the beginning it's like a seed that has germinated and as we practice we get to experience the depth of who we are which doesn't seem to have any boundaries. I look at it as tending to my inner garden which has infinite possibilities. The meditation is the water, soil, sunshine and fertilizer. The practice also becomes a way of pulling out the weeds of concepts which my mind is persistently creating. Meditation makes it possible for my inner garden to blossom and bear fruit. Those fruits were manifesting while I was living in the Ashram in very subtle ways, but I didn't stay the duration for those roots to go deep enough and stabilize. Now my inner garden was losing its spendor from neglect and the weeds were taking over my consciouness.

On the domestic front it seemed like my brother-in-law was hustling in one way or another. Whenever the landlady would come by for the rent he always had a story about large sums of money coming in the following week and that he would pay her a high interest for being late or he would plan on not being present when he knew that she would come by to collect. The money that he collected from the patients for either cosmetic surgery or abortions which he split with the doctors would find its way up his nose in the form of a white powder called cocaine. Man if you want to get high get some mushrooms or mescaline or some pure Sandoz LSD. Often I would accompany him when he would go to the Bottom Line Bar on the corner of Sunset Boulevard and Crescent Heights Boulevard. According to Don, this bar catered to Mafia types and hit men. For some reason I felt safe with these guys. To me they were men like other men that I've known. Also my training in the Ashram helped me to see people free of judgment and criticism and I didn't have a violent bone in my body. Sometimes Don would call me over to a chair and introduce me to some guy and say: "I told him about you and he's hurting so could you put your hands on him. So I would do this little procedure on the back of the head by the medulla oblongata and people would feel better. I never knew how it worked but I always felt a surge of energy going through my body when I did this and so would they. One time when I was sitting at the bar nursing a scotch on the rocks one of the guys I had treated walked up

114

to me and whispered in my ear: "If anybody ever bothers you just let me know and I'll take care of it for you." I thanked him for his offer. I knew what he was referring to and irregardless of his offer I felt protected. I also never had to pay for a drink at this bar. Somebody was always offering me a drink. Sometimes it was an offer of a watch or a woman or whatever I wanted. Basically my wants were pretty simple so I often graciously declined. I also knew that this was their culture and again no judgements.

I often had a picture of Maharaji on my shirt or lapel or sometimes it was a medallion with his picture on it hanging around my neck. One day when I was sitting at the Bottom Line Bar a man I had begun a conversation with looked at my medallion and asked: "Who is that?"

"Guru Maharaji," I responded.

"I met him. He was on the Merv Griffin Show a few years ago and I was the warm up comic. I had been in my dressing room smoking a joint and I thought the door was locked when he walked in. It surprised me and I blurted out 'Jesus Christ' and he said: 'no it's Guru Maharaji.' Something happened to me after that because something in my heart got stirred but after awhile I forgot about it." Danny, the comic, would often be at the bar when I would come with Don.

Notwithstanding the fact that my healing clinic was not opening, I wasn't anxious about it. In time I told myself that it was just a pipe dream and it wasn't going to happen. I got the impression that many promises were from a delusional mind so I gave up on it. I was having an adventure of my life and I road that wave as long as it lasted.

One day Fran, the ex Las Vegas showgirl coke dealer, who was a friend of my sister asked me to escort her to Rod Steiger's fiftieth birthday party at a mid-eastern restaurant in West Hollywood. You know those establishments where you sit on pillows on the floor by a round table and they cover the table with twenty different types of food.

"Sure," I said.

"We'll have to go and buy you some proper clothes first."

"OK with me but I don't have any money to buy clothes."

"Leave it to me. I'll take care of it," Fran said.

Huguette, my sister overheard us and she said: "I'll put some body in your hair. It will look good on you." So Fran and I went shopping for a pair of slacks, a shirt to match and some new shoes. When we got back Huguette, who had been a professional hairdresser asked me if I was ready for a change. Since my personal appearance wasn't something that I fretted about since I had been in high school I was ready for anything. When she started putting rollers in my hair and then covered them with some awful smelling solution which smelled like the permanent hair solution my mother and sisters used a long time ago, I started to get worried. When I mentioned my concern I was told that she was just putting body in my hair, so I relaxed. After a couple of hours when the rollers were taken out and I had a mirror held in front of me, I was aghast. I looked like I could pass for a Beverly Hills Jew. Not that there was any thing wrong with that. Curly hair was not something that I had ever imagined for myself. It took me a few minutes to get used to it and then the preparations to go to Rod Steiger's fiftieth birthday party got under way.

I dressed up in my new duds and then my brother-in-law loaned me a medallion to wear. My transformation from a monastic to a worldly person was just about complete.

As Fran and I started to leave the house for the party, Huguette gave me a last inspection and unbuttoned the three top buttons of my shirt. "You've got great chest hair, André, show it off," she said then she gave me a couple of joints for the road. When we entered the Moroccan restaurant, Fran told me to sit on a couch by a table next to five beautiful women. I was the only man at that table and my shyness showed up immediately. Fran had gone to the ladies room to snort some coke then she came back and introduced me to all the ladies even though she didn't know them then she told me to enjoy myself. My shyness vanished as we shared a joint and a familiar part of my personality surfaced that often came out when I had some pot to smoke. I became assertive and talkative. It felt like I was holding court and I conversed with the women in a very personal way. I started asking them about how they felt being there, where they were from, what was their relationship to Rod Steiger. I told them that I was just a few months out of the Ashram. Then I asked this beautiful blonde next to me if I could put my hand on her head and she said it was OK. So I told her to close her eyes and I put my hand on her head. A powerful buzz started going through my hand and I knew that she was feeling it also. The other women were watching and after about a minute I told her to take a deep breath and as she let it out I very slowly lifted my hand and she almost rose off the couch. Then she said: "Oh wow! What just happened?" "I don't know. You tell us, " I said. "Well when you put your hand on my head I saw all this light and then when you told me to take a deep breath it was as if I breathed for the first time and when you started to take your hand off my head I felt so light it felt like I was floating upwards."

"Will you do that to me?" asked another beautiful blonde with a deep cleavage.

"Sure. Come and sit next to me." (During all this time I was getting so horny being around this bevy of gorgeous women with their bulging breasts and sensual manners that the only way I could avoid jumping one of them right then and there was to continue this performance.) I proceeded to put my hand on her head also and the same thing happened:a powerful but gentle energy was buzzing in my hand and again it seemed like she was going to float off the couch.

"I'm next," said another woman sitting with the group.

Eventually, I "buzzed" everyone sitting on the couch with me and I'm getting very high beyond the reefer rush. After making her rounds and selling all her little vials of coke,

Fran came over and sat with me. The other women told her what happened and Fran said: "Oh yeah. He does that for me often." Then Rod Steiger happened to stroll by our table and Fran said: "I want you to do Rod." So she had someone bring a chair in the middle of the room and told Rod, who didn't look very happy and dressed in a bright blue Midwestern robe, to sit down on the chair. Then she said: "OK André put your hands on his head," which I did. So now there's about a dozen people watching what I'm doing and I'm starting to get uncomfortable. After I took my hands away from Rod's head, he walked away without saying anything as if he were not impressed. Since Fran had accomplished her mission, namely, selling all her cocaine she said that it was time to go. I got hugs and kisses from all the women that I had treated and was relieved to be leaving because I could barely contain my sexual arousal.

Within a few weeks after I left the Ashram and arrived in Beverly Hills, Don brought me to a gathering of ladies to introduce me and my work. How this came about I never asked I just saw it as an opportunity to do my thing. At this meeting I shared some of the work that I do including foot reflexology. Somebody in the group said: "Will you massage my feet?" It was the actress, Terry Moore. "Sure," I said. I sat on the floor and she lied down in front of me barefooted and I proceeded to give her a foot reflexology massage and narrated what I was doing in the process: "Now I'm touching the heart points, and the liver and now the solar plexus." "I can feel some buzzing in my solar plexus," Terry said. After the meeting was over, I met the lady who had arranged for me to be there and invited me to have lunch the following day with a friend of hers, a model.

The following day I met this lady accompanied by Susan, a beautiful tall model at a chic Beverly Hills restaurant. The lunch was to have Susan check me out to see if I was legit or a charlatan. I was quite stricken by Susan's beauty and poise. She also

ONE MAN'S SEARCH FOR THE DIVINE

owned a gracefulness that I had experienced only once and that was with Maharaji's wife. The luncheon became an opportunity for me to talk about my background as a monastic and the training I had in reflexology and other modalities I picked up on the way. Don had given me enough money to pick up the tab and so the women were impressed. Before we parted I asked for Susan's phone number and we went our separate ways.

The feelings that Susan had stirred within me had me bewildered. I had been with many women but had not felt the kind of intense attraction with Susan since my first love at the age of sixteen. It wasn't just physical although I couldn't deny the physical attraction. It wasn't lustful either. There is a feeling in the solar plexus that one feels sometimes which might be hard to describe but it's like a balloon filled to the breaking point. Psychologists call it the romantic phase which creates endorphins that can be triggered just by the person's name or picture or thoughts of that person and it certainly described my condition. It goes without saying that I called her to see if I could see her and to my good fortune she accepted.

Sometimes it's difficult to understand certain feelings that are so intense that they can demand constant attention. The professionals call it hormones or some other neurochemical but these explanations don't satisfy the soul. The only thing that makes sense is the constant longing. It can at times be obsessive. Sometimes the longing to be with someone can verge on lunacy. If it is chemical it is one of the most potent drugs impacting a human being and I was totally hooked. One time when I tried to call Susan her line was busy for three days. I imagined that she kept her phone off the hook because she didn't want to see me. There was no logic behind those thoughts. There had not been any strife in the relationship. So I drove over to her place and I was willing to use a ladder and climb over her second floor porch and force myself into her apartment if she wasn't going to open up the security gate. I was observing this insanity that I was experiencing and it didn't seem like I could control it or stop it. When I got to Susan's the security phone number was also busy. I saw that her car was parked in her space so I yelled for her. She came out to the porch and I told her that I had been trying to reach her for three days and she said that there was a problem with her phone lines. I was invited up to her apartment and with some chagrin told her what I had been going through. She was very empathic then told me that perhaps what happened triggered some past memory.

As we talked I realized that what got triggered was my feelings of abandonment when I was seven years old. My parents had moved to the United States from Canada and I had to stay behind and live with my grandmother for the first six months or until my school year was finished. It had been a raw emotional wound which had never been healed and the thought of Susan not wanting to see me brought all that

118

to the surface. I had been close to becoming a raving maniac and losing it. I think it put Susan off because she told me that she couldn't help me with my pain and that I should go a bit deeper in meditation to get some clarity. So I spent some time in the next week in meditation to allow myself to go to the source of the burning pain that I was feeling in my chest and it wasn't and ulcer or acid reflux either.

What I discovered to my surprise was my own abandonment. It was the deep pain that I had experienced most of my life that drove me to become an addict in the first place. First it was with sugar. On Sunday afternoons my mother would often make sucre à crème, a fudge made with brown sugar, white sugar, evaporated milk, vanilla extract, some butter and pecans or walnuts. I know the ingredients because I learned how to make it and when she wasn't up to it I would make it. I would hover over the container of sucre à crème to make sure that there would be plenty left over. Then what was left would find its way into my bedroom. When my parents would tell me it's time to go to bed, I never bickered because I had my stash next to my teddy bear waiting for me. My teddy bear was my alter ego and not only a great source of comfort but also indulged with me as I shared my stash with him. I would eat a piece of candy for myself and for him also, then fall asleep. If it wasn't sucre à crème, it was cookies or Ritz Crackers with peanut butter. Often times my bed had crumbs and peanut butter smeared all over my pillow case. My pillow even smelled like peanut butter. One time when I was living in Colebrook, New Hampshire someone had given me a dollar for something I had done and I went immediately to the local store and spent the whole dollar on candy bars. That's when candy bars were a nickel and you could get a 1/4 pound Baby Ruth for a dime. I still remember the feeling that came over me while I was selecting the different candy bars to purchase. It was like my observant self watching and it was saying: "Wow. You are spending the whole dollar on candy!" It didn't feel judgmental. Just making an observant statement.

When candy wasn't available there was always some form of alcohol. Beer was my favorite and when that wasn't available I always knew where my parents stashed their liquor. It always amazed me that my parents never noticed that someone was siphoning off their liquor. If they did notice they never mentioned it to us kids. Of course as I grew older my addictions expanded to sex, pornography, masturbation, tobacco, and eventually marijuana, and psychedelics. It was all to avoid feeling the pain of alienation with myself, the abandonment of self which can happen in early infancy. It is often described as a void or emptiness in the solar plexus. With what I know now, it seems to me that the pain is really my soul asking me to pay attention and what I had learned to do instead was to not only ignore the feeling but do whatever I could to numb it. In a way it's no different than a young child trying to get his mother's attention and as she continues ignoring his signals he goes and bites her on the leg to get what he wants. I've seen this happen and it always amuses me when I observe it because I know exactly what's going on. In many cases the mother doesn't have a clue about the inherent needs of her child. So this is our plight as human beings: trying to make sense of our body's pure language.

So I see that I've gotten sidetracked again. These experiences are not isolated or compartmentalized they parallel our lives daily.

After some time my relationship with Susan took a different path. I came to realize that it could never be exclusive. I could never give her the kind of life style that she wanted. It's not that she wanted so much but that I still had a lot of work to do before I could have a solid relationship with a woman. Keeping it light and occasional was best for both of us. Susan enjoyed going to Satsang with me at times or I would see her at the hall on Larchmont by herself. Ultimately she received Knowledge. We remained good friends until she died of breast cancer around the age of sixty. One of the great gifts that Susan gave me was introducing me to Saint Germain in the books by Godfre Ray King. She had some of the original books autographed by King. Some of the material I wasn't ready for and was recently reacquainted again with the material through my training in Body Electronics.

Meanwhile, the situation at my sister's house was degenerating rapidly. She and her husband's drug induced illusions could no longer sustain any sense of normalcy. The fighting became constant and the environment was too difficult for me so I moved out. I still kept working in their office doing pregnancy testing and consulting with people wanting cosmetic surgery. The only time that I saw my sister or her husband was at the office. I was fortunate to find a bachelor apartment in Hollywood across from Paramount Studios on Melrose just a few blocks east of Larchmont. This was a perfect place for me and only $115 a month which included electricity and water. I could walk from my apartment to the Satsang hall on Larchmont only about a mile away.

About a month after I moved in, Huguette told me about Danny Profit, the comic I had met at the Bottom Line Bar, needing someone to take care of him because he was disabled since he had broken his leg and had no place to live because he couldn't pay his rent. I hesitated for two or three days then gave in to the Good Samaritan within me and had him move in to my one room bachelor apartment. To this day I'm not sure if it was a mistake or a good thing to do. One thing is certain: it was never boring being with Danny.

He was about five-foot five and looked like an overweight Satyr. Growing up in a Jewish neighborhood in Brooklyn made him street smart and also contributed to his sense of humor which always amused me even though sometimes it was a bit caustic. For instance in paying cash for something he would always ask if the person took cash. It was his way of connecting with people. To this day I use that expression when I pay with cash. Most people get it but it seems like some don't. He had a lot of friends, most of them a bit shady which I found fascinating like characters in a book. Danny was collecting food stamps and receiving disability so between the two of us we managed well. Also Danny had a great source for killer pot so getting stoned was very much a daily occurrence. He would often call me on how serious I took life and that I should lighten up a little. Also he was never reluctant about expressing himself.

One time at the Satsang hall there was a premie speaking about the benefits of practicing meditation and she kept saying: "It's like you know blah blah blah and you know and you know." About ten minutes into this discourse, Danny who was a few rows behind me stood up and said: " Excuse me, excuse me. I just want you to know that I've been sitting here for the last ten minutes listening to you talk and you keep saying 'you know'. I want to tell you that I DON'T KNOW, YOU KNOW? So please stop boring me with your 'you knows'." I thought I was going to fall off my seat with laughter along with about a dozen other people. I also think that he probably spoke for many people in the hall.

Being nice was not what Danny was about and if people didn't like him it didn't seem to bother him. This part of Danny was what was completely missing in my own development so I was very attracted to his demeanor. He often said to me: "André, say what's on your mind." He would irritate me to the point that I would tell him off and he would respond with: "Bravo!" Some people might not appreciate the following story in the same way that my demented sense of humor does but here goes. Danny had been interested in receiving Maharaji's Knowledge and going to the Satsang hall as often as he could which was one of the requirements at the time to show your intention. A female Mahatma, (someone chosen by Maharaji to reveal the techniques of Knowledge) was in town to help aspirants in their final preparation to receive Knowledge. I had given notice to Danny that the following day this Mahatma would be selecting aspirants for the Knowledge session and that it might be a good idea for him to avoid partying the night before and prepare himself spiritually for the Knowledge selection. Danny given the addict that he was could not pass up a party with women, booze and drugs. The following morning I tried to wake him to get him to the meeting and he was out cold so I went by myself. About two hours into the meeting the Mahatma still had not arrived but then Danny showed up looking like an unkempt lunatic. Soon after he arrived the Mahatma sent word through the MC that she didn't think anyone was ready to receive Knowledge.

ONE MAN'S SEARCH FOR THE DIVINE

I guess maybe about ten seconds went by when we all heard Danny say: "Why that fucking cunt." I thought I was going to fall off the couch with laughter along with a few others who knew of Danny's penchant for outrageous expressions. Not too long after this incident, Danny moved to Denver. No longer was he influenced by his druggy friends, he mellowed out, cleaned up his act and ultimately received Knowledge. I would see him on occasion at festivals with Maharaji and the change in his demeanor was literally like night and day. It seemed that when he was living in Hollywood he hardly ever shaved and there was always a dark cloud hanging over his head. Now even when he didn't shave there was a mellowness around him and a loving nature that I had not seen before. You might say that his rough edges smoothed out but his sense of humor was more intact then ever just not as caustic.

As I said earlier, within six months after I left the Ashram to come to California lured on a promise by my sister and her husband to open up a healing clinic for me everything had completely gone to pot literally and figuratively. They were both so strung out on drugs and alcohol that their reality never touched the ground. I was probably in denial at the beginning. If I hadn't been so naïve in all likelihood I would have seen what obviously was a couple of completely delusional flakes. I couldn't believe that I was so easily seduced. It wasn't the first time and it wouldn't be the last. By the end of October, 1975 their marriage fell apart, the business was drained financially and I decided to go to Orlando and recharge my spiritual batteries at a festival with Maharaji.

The three day festival with my teacher was inspiring and it helped me clear my mind once more. Boy it's so easy to be distracted by this world and ignore my inner world. Of the two my inner world is so much more real, secure and dependable. I keep being reminded of something Maharaji said to me many times when I would ask what I should do with my life. He would ask: "What are you doing now?" I would respond whatever I was doing at the time: usually cooking or massage. "Do you like to do that?" he would ask. "Yes," I would reply. "Then do that, " he would say with emphasis. It was always too simple for me and yet he always drew attention to simplicity.

While at the festival in Orlando, I ran into Chuck whom I had not seen in a few years. He was with a woman and her young daughter and they were all living in Santa Cruz.

After the festival he invited me to ride along with them back to Santa Cruz in their VW van. I wasn't in a hurry to get back to California so I accepted the invitation. Within an hour after we left Orlando, Chuck's lady friend, Michal, developed intense abdominal pain. By the time we got to Gainesville her pain was so severe that we took her to the hospital for observation. They did all kinds of tests on her and couldn't come up with a clear diagnosis so the medical staff suggested exploratory abdominal surgery. I had an intuition that it was a combination of constipation and gas so I mentioned it to the hospital staff and suggested an enema. They said that without knowing what was wrong they didn't want to risk such a procedure. I told her and Chuck about my intuition and proposed that we go to the local drugstore and get a Fleet enema and Michal could administer it herself which she did. Within a short while she was on the toilet letting it all go and felt so good that she asked to be discharged. There was so much resistance by the hospital to release her that Michal got dressed and walked out on her own without going through all the discharging protocol.

Within a few miles away from Gainesville the van developed engine trouble and we returned . Chuck being a master mechanic figured out that the engine needed replacing.

After consulting with a couple of garages we found a rebuilt VW engine. To change an engine on an old VW van takes about four hours. We put a milk crate under the old engine, disconnected some wires and other parts, unscrewed four bolts and dropped the engine unto the milk crate then reversed the process with the rebuilt engine and voilà we're off again. One of the good qualities that Chuck possessed and which I admired was his self-reliance. When it came to mechanical things he was never intimidated.

Something about those characteristics reminded me of my father who could take just about anything apart and put it back together. One time my father took the Maytag clothes washer apart and had pieces scattered all over the patio. He found the piece that was broken, ordered a replacement and put the washer back together without leaving out any pieces. The washer continued working for another ten years.

We chugged back to Santa Cruz. I say chugged because with three adults, a child and baggage, the load was pretty heavy for a 38 horsepower engine and climbing some of the long hills in New Mexico was a strain on the engine. Sometimes Chuck would pull up very close to the back of a semi on the highway and cruise on the trucks pull. I stayed with Chuck and Michal in Santa Cruz for about a week while I checked out some possible gigs for myself but nothing panned out so I hitch-hiked back to Los Angeles. By the way Michal never had abdominal pains again.

I returned to my apartment across from Paramount studios. The following day I got a job as a security guard at ABC studios in Hollywood. The pay was lousy, just a quarter above minimum wage but it was a paycheck and my overhead was minimal. The scene at ABC studios was something that I had never experienced before. They taped many different shows for television. Lawrence Welk taped his shows there and whenever my mother's friends or family were in town from Quebec, I would get show tickets for them.

One time on my mother's birthday I accompanied her to the taping of the show and we danced on camera. She loved it. Welcome Back Kotter was also being taped there as well as General Hospital. One time I had the occasion to be on staff for the taping of the third season of the Dean Martin Roast. I had a chance to walk around prior to the taping so I took the opportunity to visit the celebrities on the show at their dressing rooms.

The first one I visited was Orson Wells. He looked pretty heavy and was suffering from a bad case of gout and could barely walk. We chatted for a few moments but I could see that he was in pain and not keen on conversation. The next celebrity was Gene Kelly. The energy with him was just the opposite to Orson Wells, he was enthusiastic, smiling and congenial, very much the same facial expressions as he had in the movie Dancing In The Rain. Paul Lynde was next and he seemed shy and withdrawn and appeared to be in a bad mood. After I got to talk to Joey Bishop I was told to mind my own business, leave the guests alone and perform my duties which was just to stand around and prevent stragglers from wandering around. Other celebrities were Muhammad Ali, Foster Brooks, Ruth Buzzi, Howard Cosell, Angie Dickinson, Senator Barry Goldwater, Senator Hubert Humphrey, Gabe Kaplan, Rich Little, Dick Martin, Dan Rowan, Nipsey Russell, and James Stewart. The Roastmaster was Don Rickels and the celebrity they were roasting was Dean Martin. Rickles must have done about forty five minutes and by the time he was done my sides were hurting from laughing. He roasted everybody not only Dean Martin.

When I worked the graveyard shift we had to patrol a certain area once an hour. One time when I was on that shift and patrolling I walked through one of the studios that had a sound proof room. I decided to experiment in the room by closing the door and turning out the lights. Within a couple of seconds the effects of sense deprivation made me dizzy and I became disoriented . I knew that if I stayed longer I would lose it completely.

My awareness of space and time became non-existent and I rushed out of their. It was very similar to some acid trips I had been on. During the following patrols I was always tempted to go back into that sound proof room and just trip out until someone found me the following morning. My time as a security guard was mostly pretty boring except for sitting in on some of the shows while they were being taped but eventually the lack of challenge took over and I often fell asleep on the job.

I had been told that Children's Hospital in Hollywood offered a degree in Physical Therapy. So one morning after my graveyard shift I went to their administration office to get an application for their Physical Therapy program. I already had my bachelor's degree so continuing on to get my PT certification shouldn't take too long, I thought to myself. As I was leaving the hospital with my application in hand I crossed the street to the Presbyterian Hospital side. I was walking towards Vermont Ave. and Sunset Blvd. to catch my bus home. I was starting to feel the fatigue from having been up all night and contemplated walking through the bushes and across the hospital parking lot. I never made it to the bus stop.

At approximately 9:30AM on August 25th 1976 I suddenly found myself blacked out and struggling to get up. The pain in my knees was so intense that I fell back down and a little voice in my head said: "You just got hit by a car. Go into Holy Name, relax and you'll be OK." Holy Name was one of the meditation techniques I practiced. I knew exactly what that message meant and I went into Holy Name, saw my body stretch on the sidewalk and I went into the light.

The experience in the light was Divine. There was no thought of "Am I dead?" or any other thoughts of family or life on this planet. Nothing but light not like a light from the sun or a light bulb, not like a light that you see through the eyes but a light that is all around: front, back, up, down. Actually there was no up down, front, back it was like I was the light it was a feeling that can't be described because it didn't seem like a human feeling. There were no tunnels with family and friends greeting me. Just light. Apparently in that state, time and space is non-existent so I don't know how long I was in that consciousness when that same familiar voice again said: "Open your eyes now." And I did. I was on my back looking up at a perfectly blue sky. The first two words that came out of my mouth was: "Oh wow!" Then: "Who hit me?"

A tiny lady of about seventy came over very freaked out and in shock said it was she and that she was sorry. I told her not to worry and that I would be OK. There was a crowd of people around in what seemed in a frozen state of trauma. They were looking at me and no one was making any attempt at all to comfort me. My legs were bent and my knees were in extreme pain. I asked a young girl near my feet to straighten out my legs and she said that she was afraid to. So I asked her to hold my feet while I straightened out my legs and she did. Then some yahoo from the hospital came over and apologized about not being able to help me until I was inside the hospital so I asked him to get me some ice to put on my knees.

A few minutes later he came back with two bags of ice and with much apology laid them next to me and I took them and put them on my knees myself. He

125

ONE MAN'S SEARCH FOR THE DIVINE

wasn't even allowed to do that for me. I had to take charge of my own care because everybody else were too frozen with trauma to help me.

A policeman came over and told me that they had called an ambulance even though I was less than a hundred feet from the emergency entrance to the hospital. They could have brought over a gurney and put me on it and wheel me into emergency, but no, they had to follow the rules. I realized right then and there that I couldn't go into victim mode because the real victims were the people around me who acted totally helpless. The cop asked for my identification. While laying on the sidewalk with an obvious concussion I had to take out my wallet and look for my driver's license. As the cop was copying the information from my license the ambulance arrived. The driver checked me out then asked me for my ID and I told him to get it from the cop but he told me that he had to get it from me. I reached into my back pocket again and took out my driver's license and handed it to him. In the mean time, the other two attendants put me on a gurney and slid me into the ambulance. Once the doors were closed they drove about a hundred feet to the emergency dock and gave me back my ID and wheeled me into the hospital emergency room. More surprises were waiting for me there.

The receiving attendant asked for my ID and then for my insurance card. I told her that I didn't have insurance. She asked me if I had any money. I had about thirteen dollars in my pocket and told her that she could have that. Her jaw dropped and it seemed that the energy got sucked out of the room. The chief clerk came in and told me that they would have to call an ambulance and transport me to USC General Hospital since I had no insurance or money. She said that it would be about an hour wait. I asked to talk to the chief administrator of the hospital. When she asked why, I told her that I wanted x-rays taken right away to get and exact diagnosis of the condition of my knees. They got permission to give me x-rays and wheeled me into the cold x-ray room. Once they finished taking x-rays they left me there without any covers and I began chattering uncontrollably because my body was in shock. I was all by myself in this room and felt cold and very vulnerable in what seemed like an uncaring world. I started to sing French songs that my mother had taught me when I was a little boy to soothe myself. Eventually, the ambulance arrived and after giving them my ID I was put on a gurney and wheeled into the ambulance.

On our way to USC General Hospital, I had an attendant with me. He asked me if I was married and when I said no he told me that he was. Then he started complaining about his wife and in-laws. I told him to shut the fuck up that I was the victim here and I was the one who needed some consoling and he didn't say a word until we got to the hospital.

Apparently August 25 was not a good day for a lot of us. The hospital was receiving a record number of accident victims and I was at the low end of the totem pole to receive care since my injuries were minimal compared to other victims. I got x-rays again and the technician said that so far I was the least injured of anyone he had seen that day. I guess that was suppose to cheer me up, but it didn't. After x-rays, I was wheeled into a hallway to await a trauma surgeon. About eleven o'clock that night a surgeon finally came to seeme with apologies and told me that I probably wouldn't be examined until morning. I asked him if maybe they could just drain my knees since they had become swollen like basketballs. A few minutes later another doctor came with a needle and drained my knees and put my legs in a cast right away and told me that I was good to go. I was given a pair of crutches, a prescription for some pain killers and was told to come back in a month. I called my sister Huguette to come and pick me up. We picked up the prescription on our way to her house where I spent the night and slept like a baby.

The following day, I called my girlfriend, Francis, and she picked me up and took me to her place where I played up my situation to the hilt. I went on disability and Medicaid right away and started collecting food stamps. I got in contact right away with the insurance company of the driver who hit me. The agent said that the driver was seventyfive years old and on her way to do volunteer work at the hospital when she lost control of her car and jumped the curb and hit me across the back of the knees and stopped on a tree. I had never seen the car coming because I had my back to the street and when I got hit my head hit the side walk and I suffered a concussion. The agent said that the driver had a limited policy, whatever that meant.

My friends kept telling me that I would need a lawyer to settle with the insurance company which to me didn't make sense since this case was a no brainer. I was a pedestrian on the sidewalk as far away from the curb as you can get and some car comes along right where I'm standing and jumps the curb and knocks me down. Eventually, I broke down after so many people told me that insurance companies are evil and that I would get screwed if I didn't get a lawyer so I finally called one that was referred to me by a friend that I trusted.

About a week after my accident, I called this lawyer and told him who had referred me and what happened. He told me that he would send me some papers to sign and he referred me to a doctor. The guy wouldn't even come to my place to see me. Then I went to the doctor that he referred me to and by the time this doctor was going to finish with me I would be so inconvenienced and he would have worked up such a large bill that there probably wouldn't be much left for me to collect. That afternoon, I called the lawyer and released him from the case then I called the insurance agent and told him that I was not getting a lawyer but if he tried to screw me

ONE MAN'S SEARCH FOR THE DIVINE

I would get one and it would cost his company twice what I would ask for and he understood. Now that I had all this business settled I could go back to my new life on crutches and experience what that was like.

One of the healing techniques that I had learned was to use the energy which emanates from the palms of my hands and placed them on both sides of the cast and let the energy penetrate to the damaged ligaments and tendons. I wasn't sure if this was working or not but it seemed to feel good whenever I did it. Also, I stayed quite mobile during all this time and didn't let my condition limit my activities, however, the casts were a major impediment to my sex life. It took some creative maneuvering but when the need is there we learn to adapt.

At the end of September, I went back to USC General Hospital for my first check up and they had no record of me so we had to start all over again. I had to tell them what, when and where all this happened. They took x-rays again and told me to come back in a month. I went back at the end of October and again the hospital didn't have my records so I went through the same procedure as the month before and was told to return in another month. Just before Thanksgiving I started to feel like I'm healed enough to have the casts taken off my legs and anyway the novelty had worn off. So back to USC General. Again they didn't have my records and again we started all over. This time I told them that I wanted the casts taken off and the doctor said that they would have to replace them with smaller casts. I told them that I was healed and didn't want another cast. The hospital gave me release papers to sign so that they would not be liable and the casts were removed. Once they were off the doctor bent my knees to test the flexibility. There was some slight discomfort and I was released with high fives.

Now I needed my medical records for the insurance company. Every time I went to the desk to see if my records were ready I was told that they weren't ready. Every fifteen minutes I went to the desk to check and no sign of my records. They must have gotten irritated with me because the third time I went to the desk they walked away and while I was standing there I noticed my records on top of a wire tray and I picked them up unnoticed. The people at the desk continued to ignore me so I walked away with my records and no one said a word. To this day I have no idea if the hospital has any record that I was ever there. On my way home, I was elated. I'm healed. I could walk without crutches. Making love will be unencumbered again. It doesn't get any better.

On December 15th I got my last disability check and it was just a partial of what I was getting and I was thinking: "Christmas is coming, then there's New Years eve and then rent on the first of January." I panicked for a moment. Then that familiar voice came in and said: "Spend it." I called my sister Huguette and told her that wanted to take her and my mother to lunch at Ivy's in Beverly Hills. Well, I blew my whole check on lunch and my sister had to take care of the tip. The next day the insurance agent called me and told me that he got the OK to settle. I told him that I was busy but that I could see him the next day. On the 19th, he showed up at my place and told me that he had been given permission to give me an amount that was just $500 less than what I was going to settle for so I took it. I signed the release papers and received a check which I deposited right away. When the check cleared the bank withdrew all my money in $100 bills and had a marvelous Christmas. In a little less than four months since my accident I had settled with the insurance company without lawyers, extra doctors or unnecessary hassles. My knees recovered completely with no scar tissue and I've never been bothered by them. And by the way I was so grateful to the driver of the car for hitting me. You see I had been in a deep rut for about a year and prayed every day for help and that accident catapulted me out of my rut in ways that I never could have imagined. Thank you Lord.

With my new found wealth I could afford to fly my daughter, Michelle, to visit me for the holidays and I gave her and Kim my sister Huguettes's daughter and my girlfriend Francis's daughter a C note each ($100 bill). They were all adolescent girls and had a blast shopping for themselves. I bought myself a used VW hatch-back and by the end of February I was broke again. During this time, I had vacated my apartment and crashed either with my sister or with my girlfriend.

Now I had to go look for a job but what to do? I decided to go to an agency and pass myself off as a gourmet chef for domestic employment. While being interviewed by an agent, Mrs. Jack Warner called asking for a cook for her domestic staff. "I have just the right person here for you," I heard the agent say. Then she asked me if I would be willing to be picked up and interviewed for the job and I agreed. About a half hour later an Asian American women picked me up and took me to the Warner estate in Beverly Hills for an interview with Mrs. Warner. I guess I qualified because she hired me on the spot. I was to get room and board plus $500 a month to prepare meals for the staff. Sounded good to me.

I took the job and was immediately escorted to a hacienda on the premises. It had a bedroom, small kitchen/living room with a TV and a bathroom with shower. I called my sister, Huguette to come and pick me up so that I could get my personal belongings and my car then returned to my new home on an ten acre walled in estate with two twentyfour hour security guards and a security dog. The following day I became acquainted with the staff and the kitchen. The staff consisted of Mrs. Warner's personal maid who was French, a Mexican butler, his wife who was also one of the house maids, another Asian housemaid and a couple of grounds keepers and one gardener and a little old Mexican woman who cooked Mexican food exclusively. She

ONE MAN'S SEARCH FOR THE DIVINE

was a bit shorter than five feet, very thin and looked to be about seventy-five year
old. She treated me like I was her son. There was nothing that she wouldn't assist me
with. She clued me in on all the idiosyncracies of the staff and warned me about Mrs
Warner's personal French maid.

Although I had cooked for as many as thirty people before in the Ashram
it was vegetarian cooking and I had not cooked the average American meal in year
so I had to adapt very quickly to the new Cuisine. The first meal I cooked was two
chickens with vegetables and rice. It turned out that the ovens were not working
properly that day which we found out when after an hour the chickens were barely
done. I guess the butler realized that I was a bit disoriented because he took over and
finished the chickens in the butler's pantry oven. All the staff was very helpful to me
and I could turn to them for whatever help I needed.

I had been there about two weeks when I was told that the second butler quit
and was asked by Mrs. Warner's personal secretary if I would be interested in being
the butler. I said: "sure." What I didn't know was that there had been two butlers: Jose
the Mexican butler and a young gay guy that I hardly saw who was also a butler. I had
no idea what a butler did but I was willing to learn. Jose showed me the butler's pantry
and around the first floor of the house. The upstairs was off limits except when Mrs
Warner summoned you. He told me to keep busy even if it means just walking around
the downstairs.

In the first few days of my new role as butler number 2, I stayed mostly in
the butler's pantry. There were crystal red and white wine glasses that probably had
not been used in awhile because they were dusty and smudged so I proceeded to wash
them. Not being familiar with the delicateness of thin crystal, when I wiped them dry
after washing I broke either the bowl or the stem. I must have broken a half dozen
before I got the hang of it. The broken glasses went into the garbage can. What
didn't know was that Mrs. Warner's personal maid checked the garbage can in the
pantry on a daily basis and a few days later I was told by Mrs. Warner that I should
let them know when I break something so that they could replace it. There was no
scolding about breaking the glasses just about not reporting it.

After about a week, all the crystal in the pantry had been washed so I started
to explore the different rooms on the first floor. Each room was quite unique. The
main living room had many art pieces including a portrait of Mrs. Warner by Salvador
Dali and busts by Rodin. The dining hall had a long table that sat about thirty people
I imagine at times when Jack was well that this place was buzzing with activity. The library had many metaphysical books and all the original screenplays including Camelot
which Warner Brothers produced. Since I had seen the movie a couple of times

found reading the screenplay quite fascinating. It seemed that not much attention was paid to my daily activities so I wandered around the property, inside and outside, on a daily basis. There was a huge green house with many different types of roses and orchids that I found quite delightful. This was the source of the many fresh cut flowers which appeared in the main house every day.

In spite of the fact that I lived in such opulence, I found it boring and going to Satsang at the Larchmont hall in the evening helped me to stay centered. My "disappearance" at night though was not convenient for Mrs. Warner and I was told that if I wanted to leave the premises at night I had to clear it with her first as she might need my services. I got her to agree to give me at least three nights a week for my spiritual needs. I knew, that because of conversations with her on the subject of spirituality, that she would be more open to my needs for Satsang. One time Maharaji had a program in Denver that I wanted to attend. So I asked her if she would give me the time off and advance me the money to fly there and to my great delight she not only gave me the time off but also contributed to my airline ticket. She was very gracious to me in many ways and I often appealed to her sense of spirituality. She had a way of being a bit crass with me at times. One time I said to her: "Mrs. Warner, I know that the way you are talking to me is not your usual manner and I find it upsetting so I would appreciate it if you would speak to me in a kindly manner." She apologized and never spoke to me again in a crass way. I can't say that she was so kind in the way that she spoke to others. I imagine that her life must have been quite despairing for her with her husband being so feeble after his second heart attack and the life style that she had once known was no longer possible. I had a lot of compassion for her while still maintaining my boundaries.

I had been there about three months when the demands on my time became more and more to the point where I could not attend Satsang except for one day on the week-ends. I could never understand Mrs. Warner's need to have me available in the evening because all I did was sit around just in case she needed me which was infrequently. So one day I confronted her and told her that I could no longer work for her under these conditions.

I wasn't getting any more money for being available almost twenty-four hours a day and it wouldn't make any difference to me if she did pay me more, I wanted to have at least three nights a week off. She eventually told me that if I wasn't willing to be available to her every night that she would have to let me go without any hard feelings. We parted amicably.

Within a few days after I left the Warner residence I learned that Maharaji was giving a three day festival in Montreal in June, this was in 1976. I announced at

ONE MAN'S SEARCH FOR THE DIVINE

the Satsang hall that I would be driving to Montreal for the event and had space for one other passenger to share gas expense. The only person that responded to my announcement was Sally, a single mother with a baby boy not yet a year old. Sally often sang her own songs accompanying herself with her guitar at these evening Satsang events and I always liked her voice but had difficulty with her personality, but since she was the only applicant I suspended my judgments and took her and her baby boy on. Before we were out of the Los Angeles city limits my impression of her had already changed and I found her quite likable. Our first stop in our VW hatchback was Denver. I had called my friend Rennie Davis and arranged to crash at his place and freshen up a bit. The following day we drove as far as Detroit and continued on with the third leg of our trip after a good night of rest.It was at the end of our third leg that things got a little weird and defies explanation.

A few days before I left Los Angeles, I had called my uncle Donald in Montreal to ask if he could put me up while I was at the event with Maharaji. He was gracious to accommodate me and told me to call him when I arrived and he would give me directions to his home. We arrived near the edge of the city at about ten-thirty at night and pretty fatigued by then. I called uncle Donald, got directions and asked him if there was room for my companion and her child and he said fine. I got back in the car with the directions. I was to take the beltway to a certain exit and continue a few more blocks and arrive at his place. I must have been in some strange zone because I drove over an overpass turned right, went down the ramp and entered the beltway. I was the only car on the road. On the other side of the divider, there was a traffic of cars going in the same direction tooting their horns and signaling us and making very strange jesters. I still couldn't figure out what was going on when Sally said (in a calm voice): "Andre, I think you're on the wrong side of the freeway." I said: "I think your right." And instead of slowing down and making a U-turn, I started looking for an exit. About a quarter of a mile further I saw an entrance ramp which immediately became an exit ramp and I proceed to drive up the ramp. When I got to the top there were two lanes of traffic waiting for the signal to enter the ramp I was on. I made a quick right turn, crossed the overpass, made a left on the entrance ramp and entered the freeway. As I looked over to my left I could see that there was just as much traffic as on my side of the road. I had just been driving just a few minutes before in the opposite lane when the road was empty. "How could the opposite lane have been empty a few minutes before and busy now," I wondered to myself? To this day I still can't make sense of what happened. I don't know if Sally and I were both hallucinating from exhaustion or if there was some cosmic suspension of reality. I do know that I was not alone in my perception and later on whenever Sally and I got together we would bring up this incident. However, this was not the first time this kind of "hallucination" happened to me.

132

Andre Patenaude

In the summer of 1973, I was driving around Denver with friends. The car belonged to a girl who was an acquaintance of one of my friends and they were sitting in the back seat. No, they weren't making out. In the front passenger seat was another male friend. We were driving on an eastbound three lane one-way street around rush hour and I was in a hurry to get to our destination. Unfortunately, I was stuck behind one row of cars all travelling at the same rate of speed. I would go from lane to lane trying to get ahead of the cars ahead of me but none of the cars gave way so in my frustration I stayed behind the red car in the middle lane and turned to the guy in the passenger's seat and told him that I was going to just follow the traffic when the girl in the back seat who's car I was driving said: "Oh my God, you just drove through that car!" I turned to look straight ahead and to my amazement I was now in front of the red car that a few seconds ago I had been tailing. Neither the guy in the passenger's seat nor the other two guys in the back seat saw what happened. Only the girl, the owner of the car, saw what happened. We all dismissed this phenomenon as a hallucination and never talked about it.

About three weeks later some friends and I went out to dinner and I shared this experience with them. They all looked at me with some suspicion and went on to other subjects of discussion. I needed a ride home after dinner and one of the ladies with us volunteered to take me home. She was driving a VW bug and as we were approaching a six way intersection I saw that we had a red light, but there was no attempt by the driver to slow down. I had a strong sense that she was not going to stop, but I gave no warning. As we drove through the intersection, the car that had the green light and the right of way, driving very fast came through the intersection. His headlights were on my window right by my head and we kept on going. About a hundred feet later my friend said: "Did that car just drive through us?" I said: "I don't know. All I know is that I saw the car's headlights were practically on my head and nothing happened as if we were just mist." She said: "You know when you were telling me that story about you driving through that red car, I doubted that it really happened as you told it and thought that you were making all that up. And now this happened and I feel a little crazy." She took me home and every now and then when we would see each other we would bring up that incident again. So when that strange event happened on the beltway in Montreal I just chalked it up to another unexplained hallucination. The thing is in all three incidences, I was not alone.

Paranormal experiences were familiar to me. I never questioned or try to analyze them. To me it was an affirmation that there was a power beyond my human understanding that was taking care of me and I took it for granted. Until recently, sharing these events with others didn't feel safe. As a child I often had experiences that were difficult to explain, so I never shared them. I became more and more aware

133

of a "Divine" protection as a teenager when I started driving, especially when I was dating a girl who lived twenty miles from my home. Often times after I left her house in the wee hours of the morning and arrive home wondering how I got there because I was narcoleptic and often passed out. If I wasn't aware of driving then who was doing the driving?The program with Maharaji in Montreal was divine as usual and when it was finished I spent some time visiting family and telling them about my experience with Knowledge and Maharaji. Maybe it was the way I presented it but I got the impression that they thought I was going off the deep end. About a week after the program, I arranged to get passengers to help me pay for gas to drive to Denver. I had had enough with the Los Angeles area and decided to move back to Denver where I had a lot of connections. Within a few days upon arriving in Denver I found a place to live with David, a paraplegic who had a spare bedroom and needed some assistance. Being back in Denver was comforting. I had a support system there and above all my daughter Michelle lived there. While at David's, I started a small baking business and found some health foodstores and a health food restaurant to sell my whole wheat cinnamon rolls to. I also baked some croissants with a special filling and some apple strudels. Eventually, I branched off into banana nut bread, a lemon loaf and some peanut butter and chocolate chip cookies all with healthy ingredients of course.

One day while I was delivering my baked goods to one of the stores, I met Mary, who had been an acquaintance from four years before when I lived in the Ashram. She had been married and divorced with two young daughters under the age of three. We talked and caught up then she invited me for dinner. We arranged for an evening over the following weekend. When I arrived at Mary's house, she was busy in the kitchen fixing dinner while smoking a joint. She offered me a joint and we both got royally stoned. Dinner did happen in a haphazard way and after the kids went to bed Mary invited me into her bed. A few weeks later I moved in with Mary and continued my make-shift bakery in her kitchen. Mary's place became a bit crowded after awhile and we decided to find a bigger place. Again I can't seem to get away from pot and the people who smoke it. My addiction to pot and sex got refueled once more.

We found a four bedroom house with a finished basement in Wheatridge, Colorado a suburb of Denver and close to Arvada where my daughter lived. We had a room for her whenever she could visit. Not too long after we moved in, my cousin Roger and his girlfriend moved in with us. Eventually, Chuck and his girlfriend Michal and her daughter arrived from Santa Cruz, California in a large truck with a makeshift one roomhouse on the back of the cab. They also moved in. Sharing the rent with everybody made it easy because I wasn't making that much money with my baking. There was always the aroma of cinnamon mixed with the scent of pot in the house. At times, it seemed that the house was a den of pot smokers. But except for Roger's girlfriend and Chuck's girlfriend, we were all affiliated with Maharaji and we attended Satsang often, at least three nights a week and everyone helped in the production of the pastries besides indulging in them when they were stoned.

One night when I went to Satsang by myself, I saw Sally who was now living in Denver with her son. We struck up a conversation and she invited me over to her place for some tea. Sally and I had gotten close on our trip from Los Angeles to Montreal, but our relationship had never become sexual. After she put her son to bed we had tea and she lit up a joint. We were in the bathtub together before we ever finished our tea and I never made it back to Wheatridge that night. As you can imagine it didn't fare well with Mary. I told Mary that I didn't want to be monogamous anymore and that she would have to share me with Sally. She was reluctant, but I gave her no choice. I decided that I liked being free and not "shackled" to one woman. Eventually, I struck up another affair with a woman about twenty years older. For a few weeks, having three women in my life who wanted to be with me was an amusing phenomenon. I didn't grow up in a polygamous family so I had no point of reference for juggling my schedule to please what I had decided were my women. But eventually jealousies started to peer its ugly head and it wasn't fun anymore. I had to start answering for my whereabouts. Things were degenerating rapidly where I was living also since we had difficulty meeting the rent. Eventually, we were evicted and Chuck and Michal with her daughter Jennifer and I moved into a different house with less rent.

Soon after we moved into this other house we got the news that there would be a three day festival with Maharaji in Miami on the first day of Spring. We would all be driving down in Chuck's made-up motor home. It was necessary to do some mechanical work on the truck and some renovations in the living quarters. We added an extension over the cab of the truck wide enough for a single mattress. Michal hung curtains over the windows and within a few weeks we were set to go. While all these preparations were going on, my daughter expressed a desire to go to the festival. I told her to tell her mother that she wanted to go and to ask for her blessings. Well, that didn't go over very well, I wasn't surprised when her mother would not let her miss school for an event that she didn't approve of anyway. I suggested that if she wanted to go with us that she make her own plans by getting some clothes together and that we would pick her up at a diner near her school on the morning that we were leaving. She was fourteen years old by now and it seemed to me that it was time that she took charge of her life and not be at the mercy of her mother or any other authority but herself. I knew that this decision would be contentious, but I was willing to risk it. So, according to plan, the morning we left we drove by the diner and Michelle was there waiting for us and we were on our way. I told her to call her mother around the time that she would be getting home from school to inform her of her whereabouts.

ONE MAN'S SEARCH FOR THE DIVINE

That didn't go over very well either and I told her mother that she would be safe with me and that this festival was paramount for devotees and that Michelle was also a devotee and that we would stay in touch.

The festival we were going to with Maharaji is called: "Holi." This is an ancient celebration mostly in India and known as the celebration of colors and the celebration of love.

The festival has many purposes. First and foremost, it celebrates the beginning of the new season, Spring. Hindus believe it is a time of enjoying Spring's abundant colours and saying farewell to Winter as well as a justification to reset and renew ruptured relationships, end conflicts and accumulated emotional impurities from the past. Children and youth spray coloured powder solutions at each other, laugh and celebrate, while elders tend to smear dry coloured powder on each other's face. This was not my first Holi festival, but it was Michelle's and I was excited about sharing this one with her. We arrived in Miami a couple of days before the festival began and got in touch with my cousin, Roger, who was staying in a hotel which made it convenient for us in the "motor home" as we could shower in his room. The "colors" part of the festival happened at the Orange Bowl.

The first day of the festival we all dressed in white and trucked down to the Orange Bowl stadium. There must have been about five to six thousand people attending and most were dressed in white. Weather wise it was a perfect day: temperature about 80 with a clear blue sky. Maharaji had some engineers build him a rig with a double hose that could spray colored water halfway across the field. When he arrived we could feel the excitement getting stronger and stronger. He walked over to the platform where the hoses were, turned them on and blue colored water came flying out. Everyone's white clothes were now drenched in blue water. After a few minutes, the color turned to red then to yellow. We were all jumping up and down like children with our hands up enjoying the moment of play. My inner child was completely at hand. This was an opportunity to let go of all my concepts and resistance and just play and I enjoyed it immensely along with seeing Michelle enjoying herself. Sometimes Maharaji would sprinkle flower petals or shiny sprinkles in the stream of colored water. This went on for about an hour and a half during which rock and roll music was being piped in through the PA system. To my adult mind, this event seemed over the top but to my inner-child, I was delighted.

After the festival, we drove to Gainesville and took up temporary residence in a two bedroom apartment. Gainesville is a quaint Southern college town with a population at the time of a little over 100,000 and very typically sub-tropical. There was a community of premies there so it was easy to integrate into that culture. Chuck

136

and I passed ourselves off as seasoned painters and we got jobs with a construction company. During that time, Michelle communicated with her mother in such a way that her mother found out where she was and came to Gainesville to pick her up. We said good-bye and promised to see each other soon.

Ever since I had left the Ashram and fell flat on my face spiritually, I've wanted to reenter the discipline. I would get close and then the addictive part of my personality would take over. It was a seesaw. I felt like a yo-yo and at the mercy of my seductive mind. After awhile though it was again clear that I had to make a major effort to clean up my act and with all sincerity re-apply to be accepted into the Ashram. It took another deadend relationship with another woman and seeing Maharaji again for me to commit to doing whatever it took to move into the Ashram. It wasn't the Ashram per se that was important but the discipline that helped me anchor my consciousness with my heart. I knew ultimately achieving that would carry me into a peaceful, loving and harmonious existence for the rest of my life. I had no doubts about that.

ONE MAN'S SEARCH FOR THE DIVINE

Andre Patenaude

PART III

REDEMPTION

I had volunteered many times to do food service for the large festivals with Maharaji. I enjoyed every aspect of food preparation, the baking and cooking even the planning and ordering of supplies. Many people in the organization knew about my culinary gifts and when the ten day outdoor festival in Kissimmee, Florida was scheduled for the first part of November in 1978, I was asked if I would be willing to volunteer my services for a baking project. When I was contacted for that service I knew that somehow the Universe had heard my silent pleas. We were to bake125,00 muffins for approximately 20,000 people who would be coming from all over the world. The baking would take place in New Jersey. A friend of mine who had his own bakery would be overseeing the baking for ten days at a large bakery that we leased. He also invited me to stay with him during that time.

It was such a relief to be doing self-less service again. My duties in this project were to do the mixing of the batter which would then be taken by others and put into paper muffin containers then baked, wrapped and flash frozen. We had seven different muffins to bake: blueberry, banana nut, cornbread, chocolate chip, ginger-bread, pumpkin andcarrot. I worked with a large Hobart mixer with an 80qt bowl. I had access to bins of flour, barrels of vegetable oil, raisins, walnuts, chocolate chips, spices and a 500 pound drum of unfiltered honey. We would start our day with a short meditation and some sharing about the joy of service. Again being reminded that service wasn't what we do but that it is the heart that drives the action.

For the first time in four years, I felt enthusiastic about what I was doing. True service can do that. For ten days I mixed flour, salt, baking powder, oil, honey and spices. There was a flow of energy in the bakery that already felt like the beginning of the festival. Volunteers from all over the country poured the batter in muffin pans. Others took care of the oven. Some worked with the wrapping machine and labels, some packed them in boxes then they were put into a semi freezer. One day while I was doing the mixing, I happened to be drawing from the drum containing honey and filtering out the dead bees through a strainer. I had been doing this for

139

ONE MAN'S SEARCH FOR THE DIVINE

three or four days and up until then not much thought was given to the dead bees. On this day, something in my consciousness opened up and I became in awe of the work that all the bees had made to provide all this honey. "It must have taken millions of bees and hundreds of millions of trips back and forth from the flowers to the bee-hive. That's a lot of energy," I thought. And then the thought came: "It had to take millions of flowers and a lot of rain and sunshine to produce those flowers. Nature was so generous to us by providing this nutrition." As I was contemplating these thoughts I became overwhelmed with gratitude for not only what was being provided but for the love that I was feeling and for the awareness of it all. Then I scooped out large scoops of walnuts and again the awareness of the energy that it took to manifest these nuts blew me away. This awareness of loving abundance played with me all day: with the flour, the oil, the raisins and the spices. By the end of the shift, I was in such a state of bliss that it lasted for weeks and it came back again when I was at the festival and saw people sitting somewhere and carefully opening and enjoying their muffin.

A few days after the baking was finished, I made arrangements to go to Orlando and volunteer to do service at the festival. During this time my daughter, Michelle, decided to leave her mother again and with friends drove down to Orlando for the festival. She was now sixteen and wanted to be on her own. It was a special experience for me to have my daughter with me at the festival and witness her par-ticipation and spiritual growth.Maharaji's organization had leased 360 acres of open field for the festival. A main stage for Maharaji and a smaller stage on either side was almost complete when I arrived.

There were tents everywhere for those who had chosen to stay in tents. Each tent was supplied with sleeping bags and cots. There was also a huge open tent where the kitchenwas located next to another enclosed tent serving as a dining hall. The kitchen had ten 100 gallon steam kettles sitting side by side. There were sinks and tables for preparing food. Men's and women's showers were built. There was no roof to these showers, just curtains set up in such a way that it provided privacy from the outside. There was another tent that served as a convenient store. It carried toiletries, some snacks, sandwiches, first aid items, and fresh fruit. We were expecting about 20,000 people.

When I approached the supervisory help and signed up to do service, I was assigned to be the liaison between the kitchen and the Indian delegation to provide them with whatever they needed to prepare their own food. Wow! I was going to be eating Indian food for the duration of the festival. It doesn't get any better. There were Indians from South Africa, England and India. The women were mostly dressed in their saris and some of the men wore what we call Indian pajamas, usually white or khaki. The women also brought their own spices. They told me that they didn't rust that they could find quality spices in this country. It was the greatest pleasure for me to support these ladies and to benefit from their culinary art. Each night after the main program the Indians would comeback and make chai then go to a made up stage where tablah drummers and sitar players would accompany men singing Bhajans (Hindu devotional songs) while some women would dance til they went into states of ecstasy. I felt so grateful and privileged to have been taken in by their spiritual culture.Maharaji gave two talks a day: one in the early afternoon and one in the evening. The talks happened from the stage and as this was an outdoor event we, the audience, sat on the grass on an open field. The evening talks were usually followed with music and singing. Many of the devotees have written songs expressing love and gratitude to Maharaji. Sometimes the music included popular love songs and the celebration would go on for an hour or two. It was always heartfelt and gratifying.

Something happened to me that never happened before while listening to Maharaji speak. I felt extremely anxious and agitated. There was a strong impulse to leave the premises. It was like some foreign entity was inside of me trying to get out. I had heard of stuff like this and had my doubts about it and now it was happening to me. I felt a bit insane. I found myself hanging on to the grass with both hands to prevent myself from leaving. I felt possessed. Then weird sounds started to come out of my mouth that was neither English or French. People around me would scurry away from me. When the talk was finished everything inside of me calmed down and I would go back to the kitchen to help the Indian ladies. This phenomenon happened two different times. I have no explanation for what happened. But eventually my body calmed down.

When the festival finished, I stayed on the site to help in the kitchen as we had to continue feeding those who stayed behind to clean the site and tear down the stage and the tents and showers. Soon after that I let those in charge of admitting people into the Ashram know that I wanted to be considered as a candidate. It was suggested to me that I should find a house with premies who are dedicated to the meditative way of life and move in with them and start practicing the Ashram discipline and I did just that. There was a group of guys who had been part of setting up the festival site and wanted to stay in Orlando and continue a life of service and meditation and welcomed me to live with them as the house cook. Right down my alley. I was baking bread again and preparing meals. I started sprouting alfalfa seeds and one of the guys in the house set up a whole sprinkling system for sprouting. Within a month, we were sprouting about fifty pounds of alfalfa and mung a week and selling some of it to local health food restaurants. It was also at this time that I came down with a major case of hypoglycemia. I didn't know anything about hypoglycemia at the time. Getting up in the morning became very difficult. My blood sugar would be so low that I just about had to crawl to the bathroom and pray that I could get back. I was sent to an

ONE MAN'S SEARCH FOR THE DIVINE

herbalist and was put on a heavy regimen of herbs, vitamins and minerals and in due course got stronger and stronger. One night, Michelle showed up at our house and told me that the friends that she had been staying with had kicked her out. I didn't ask any questions but also knew that she was going through her own growth. I arranged for her to stay with me for the night and let the other men know that the next day we would find some kind of solution.

The next morning I said to Michelle: "I know that you don't want to go to school and I'm not going to force you to go, but you can't stay here. This is your life and you are ultimately responsible for it. I want you to sit in the meditation room and practice for one hour and get clear. After that, you can have some breakfast then you can go and find a job. I would suggest a waitress job because you can start to make instant cash. Then find yourself a place to live. If you take the steps you need to make to take care of yourself, the Universe will fill in the blanks." And she did exactly what I told her to do. She got a job before lunch and a waitress in the restaurant who needed a roommate took her in. A month later, Michelle invited me over to her place for dinner and told me that ever since she was ten years old she had wanted a place of her own. Later she purchased a car, got her GED and went to massage school to become one of the premier massage therapist in Florida who works two days a week at the permanent Cirque du Soleil site at Disneyworld.

I had been living the Ashram lifestyle for about six months and my health had improved considerably when I heard that a cook was needed in the local men's Ashram and my name was suggested. I was very grateful and humbled by this opportunity and jumped at the chance. Within a few days, I was back in the Ashram with a deeper appreciation and conscientious dedication to the practice of spiritual Knowledge. It so happened that, at this Ashram, there was a brother there (we called ourselves brothers) that had a severe case of hypoglycemia even more formidable than mine. I now knew how to prepare food for a hypoglycemic. Mornings were either yogurt and fruit or oatmeal with a bit of honey. Sometimes he would ask for millet and tahini. Sometimes for lunch it would be just sprouted alfalfa seeds and a tahini dressing then for dinner whatever the rest of the household ate. He was also on a heavy regimen of supplements.

One day, Michael, not his real name, told me that he had been deprogrammed twice. Apparently his Jewish parents believed that we were all practicing a cult and this was the time around the Jim Jones mass suicide, and his parents feared for his life so they had this thirty year old man kidnapped and taken to an undisclosed place in Utah and had him put through some kind of deprogramming. They isolated him and physically restrained him, and barraged him with continuous arguments and attacks against his new spiritual practice, threatening to hold him forever until he agreed to

142

leave it. Michael found a way to escape and his parents had him picked up again and this time they tried to seduce him with women and money and drugs and again he escaped but had been mercilessly traumatized by it all. I later heard of other Ashram members going through the same thing.

About three months after my move into the Ashram, I was asked if I would be willing to move to Miami Beach and cook for premies who were training to be instructors for Maharaji. Of course, I accepted and a few days later someone drove me to the house in Southern Florida. I was to cook breakfast and dinner for twelve people. I had a car to drive and a pretty good size budget.

Actually the house was on Rivo Alto Island, a small island just West of Miami Beach. To get there, you had to take the Venetian Causeway from Miami Beach go through Belle Isle and turn left onto E. Rivo Alto Dr. and we were the third house on the East side. The house had enough bedrooms on the second floor to accommodate all twelve candidates. I had my own private quarters on the first floor next to the entryway. It was probably the maid's quarters at one time but private and near the kitchen. I arrived a few days before the instructor candidates to stock the kitchen pantry and refrigerator with food. The kitchen was to be strictly vegetarian so lots of tofu, brown rice, cheese, pasta and fruit and vegetables.

A few days after my arrival, the candidates arrived with much excitement and enthusiasm. Some of them I had known from having lived with them in other Ashrams. They were to meet with Maharaji for six to eight hours every day for a month. I felt quite privileged to have had the opportunity to be part of the support for their training. They always seem to glow when they would arrive after the day's session. I did my best to prepare something for dinner according to expressed desires. One day I fixed pasta with a marinara sauce and everybody raved about the dinner except the Italian candidate. He came to me after dinner and said: "You call that Italian. You have no idea what a marinara sauce is. Tomorrow I will show you how to cook Italian." I wasn't that attached to my kitchen or how someone appreciated my cooking so I welcomed his Italian expertise. The following day, he showed up for lunch with a bag of groceries containing a couple of cans of Italian tomatoes, carrots, onions, celery and basil. He chopped up some onions, carrots and celery and sauteed them in lots of olive oil while the tomatoes were cooking down. Then he mixed everything together, cooked the pasta el dente, poured the sauce over the pasta, sprinkled some chopped basil on top and said: "Now eat real Italian food. This is the way my mother made marinara sauce. Very simple." I must say that it was absolutely delicious and I've been fixing marinara sauce that way ever since.

ONE MAN'S SEARCH FOR THE DIVINE

Each day the candidates came back from spending the day with Maharaji in such a state of great enthusiasm that I resonated with it also.

I must say though that at times I felt a bit envious but I reminded myself that a great privilege was being bestowed on me by my service. Many years ago at the school Ashram, Maharaji helped us get clear on the phenomenon of service. He said: "So you think cleaning the bathrooms is service? You think that whatever you do is service? No! Cleaning the bathroom is cleaning the bathroom. Whatever you do is whatever you do. Service is what you do from your heart.

It's effortless. There is no resistance. There is a feeling of joy when you do service." I must say that it took me quite awhile for that to sink in.

When the instructor candidates were finished with their training, they were given new suitcases, a wardrobe and assignments to different parts of the world to assist Maharaji in introducing his teachings of peace and self-realization through the practice of Knowledge. A few days later, I was by myself in this large six bedroom house. In spite of being alone and not having much to do, I was still revved up from having to plan meals, shop for groceries and cook for twelve people. I was told by the Ashram coordinator to just chill and eventually they would find another assignment for me. I had a car to drive and a generous allowance so I had no concerns about my own care. I took advantage of my free time to ride my bike to the beach and read. I read the Mahabharata and the Ramayana, the two major Sanskrit epics of ancient India. Among the principal works and stories in the Mahabharata is the Bhagavad Gita. My friend, Chuck, had given me a well worn copy of The Urantia Book so I read that also. After about three weeks of leisure time I started feeling guilty and when I approached the Ashram coordinator about my feelings he told me that I had to learn to accept the moment and when the time is right I would be given an assignment. Who knew that it would be so difficult to experience leisure. I took advantage of the situation and practiced meditation, read and learned to hang out with myself.

Three weeks later I was assigned to cook at another house in North Miami Beach housing six people. My best memory of this house was the mango tree in the backyard. The fruits were in season. There's a certain magic about going out in the backyard in the morning and picking up a freshly ripened mango from the ground that had fallen during the night.

Again in this new house I had a lot of leisure time and fortunately had learnedto take advantage of it. After two months the house was disbanded and I was assigned to cook at another Ashram house in Miami Beach near the Arthur Godfrey causeway. This was to be my last assignment. It was here that I finally became emotionally stable enough to live in the world free of paranoia and fear.

144

One benefit to doing service at this house was that whenever a Mahatma (one of Maharaji's Indian instructors) came to town, he would stay at our house. Mahatma Jagdeo visited often and we would hang out together most of the time. I would pick him up at the airport, make sure that he had everything he needed. I prepared his meals, played tennis with him and chauffeured him around. With each visit, he would be invited by an Indian family for dinner and of course I was the one to assist him. They insisted that Jagdeo bring his tablas to accompany their son on the sitar. I always looked forward to these invitations because Indian food had become some of my favorites even though I sucked at preparing it myself and of course the sitar/tablas concerts were inspiring. Jagdeo always made me feel special and treated me with incredible respect and honor as did the family we visited. One time Jagdeo said to me that he could stay in any one of the Ashram houses in Miami, but he chose mine because I was there. I always looked forward to his coming.

One of my responsibilities as the Ashram housemother (that was my official title) was to assign house duties to householders. I had assigned kitchen cleaning to the youngest resident, a young man of twenty-two. Not his favorite thing to do. I would often have to remind him to do a complete job which meant wiping down the counters and the stove.

One night after coming home from a Satsang program at 9 PM, I went to check out the kitchen and nothing had been done. The person assigned to the task was sleeping. In the middle of making a mad dash towards his bedroom something in my gut stopped me and I heard in that familiar non-verbal voice: "You do it. You clean the kitchen." The message, although subtle, was so powerful that it stopped me in my tracks and I made an immediate u-turn and went back to the kitchen and started cleaning up. I spent two hours cleaning and it seemed like ten minutes. It was almost like a dance. It was a dance as I moved around the kitchen, placing the dishes in the dishwasher, washing the pots and pans and wiping down the counter and the stove and the refrigerator. It was an experience that I hold precious to this day because whenever I'm in my own kitchen which is often, I have the same feeling: a feeling of joy and freedom and free of resistance. You might say it is a sense of true service.

Almost a year after moving into this last Ashram house I started feeling like it was time to go into the world on my own. I spoke to the Ashram coordinator about my feelings and he told me to take my time. I was to secure a job and a place to live before moving out. I had waited on tables in the past and was sure that it was something that I could do again so after breakfast I would go out with the local want ads and apply to the restaurants on the list. In all honesty, I would apply at restaurants that I didn't particularly want to work in but my inner programming did not honor my feelings. It didn't matter if I didn't like a place, I had to get a job. I did this for two weeks without getting any callbacks. On one Monday morning, I picked up the Sunday want ads and took off again looking for work. Again I came home that afternoon without a job. Tuesday morning as I was walking out the door with the newspaper in my hand, that familiar voice showed up again and said: "Take me with you." That voice was so strong that it stopped me in my tracks again and I realized that I wasn't considering my feelings when I was applying for jobs. It had been more like rowing upstream towards something I didn't want. That day I drove past many restaurants where the day before I would have applied for work and I walked in and out of other restaurants without filling out a job application. I came back to the Ashram that afternoon without having filled out any job applications and I was ecstatic. The feeling was more like I had gone out to play rather than looking for work.

There was no pressure to get a job except the pressure I put on myself. That evening before going to bed I looked at the want ads again from the Sunday paper and this time I saw a large ad that I had not noticed before. The ad was for Dominique's Restaurant, a four-star restaurant, opening soon at the luxury Alexander hotel on Miami beach.

Somehow I had missed that ad perhaps because I was looking at the smaller three line ads anyway I called the number displayed and made an appointment for an interview. This time I took the bus since it was on the bus line. So far so good.

The hotel was quite impressive with its grand entrance and staircase made of cherry wood leading up to the restaurant. Finishing touches and detailing were still going on with the banquet seating. The maitre'd was a young perhaps twenty-five year old tall, slim very good looking man with an appealing smile. His welcome was pleasant and warm with a sparkle in his eyes. I filled out a job application form. The last time I had worked as a waiter was as a student in college so I had no references. He asked me questions relating to wine and my knowledge of bar drinks. I was totally clueless. When the interview was finished he said that he would call me when they made a decision. I left without giving it much thought and took the bus back to the Ashram. The next day the maitre'd called and asked me to come in again for another interview. In the second interview, he said that my qualifications were lacking but that they still wanted to hire me because he liked my demeanor and would train me and when can I start. I told him that I could start immediately. The restaurant wouldn't open for another two weeks, but there were many preparations that needed to be done and if I was willing to help I would get paid for my services. I was hired immediately.

The next day, I showed up in my working clothes and was told to take the van and pick up some boxes at the air freight terminal. For two weeks, I did a bunch of odd jobs, unpacking boxes of dishes, silver salt and pepper shakers, expensive ash trays, kitchen supplies, and special napkins and table cloths.

A few days before the grand opening, all the waiters showed up and we were paired up as teams. One of the waiters was a friend of mine who had been hired and we decided to partner up. He would work the front and I would work the kitchen meaning that he would be the first one to greet the guests as they sat down and I would get the drink orders. My partner would describe the specials to the guests, take their food orders, turn them over to me and I would place the orders in the kitchen and bring out the food. The front man always had to be in sight of the tables assigned so that if anyone needed something they would get immediate attention.

Dominique's was the namesake of Dominique d'Ermo who had another very successful restaurant by the same name in Washington D.C. His restaurant had often catered the White House during the Nixon years. Dominique was present on our first day of training and spoke with a thick French accent. He said that the client is the reason that we have a job and that it was our duty to always please the client. We never say "no" to the client and if he wants scrambled eggs and toast for dinner that is what we prepare for him. We never say: "I'm not your waiter. We are everyone's waiter. Be like a Polaroid, have instantaneous recognition of what the client needs," he would say. I really felt good about this man and besides he was French. In my four years of working for Dominique, I got to know him well. Besides working for him as a waiter, I was also his massage therapist. The following are a few facts about him along with my personal experience. Dominique d'Ermo had started his career in the hospitality industry as a pastry chef, but had gradually moved upwards to become the Food and Beverage Director of the Shoreham Hotel in Washington, D.C., before opening his restaurant in 1974. At that time, Washington was considerably less cosmopolitan than it is now and Dominique had little competition in the classy restaurant category, other than perhaps the Sans Souci, near the White House, on 17th Street, which closed in 1985. Serving exotic game dishes like venison or boar, rattlesnake salad and alligator steak, was a notable part of his menu.

Dominique travelled between Washington, DC and Miami making sure that his restaurants were operating according to his standards. Of course in the winter during the heavy tourist season in Florida I saw him often. Not long after I started working I told him about my massage experience and he began booking massages with me. We can learn much about a person's history from their bodies. One day while I was massaging Dominique's face, he was squinting uncontrollably and expressed major discomfort. I asked him what was going on and he related a story about having joined the French resistance as a teenager during WW II and blowing up bridges. He was captured by the Germans and scheduled to be executed along with other prisoners. He said that he had been tied to a tree and punched in the face. As the SS was getting ready to open fire on the prisoners, a German army officer arrived and asked to see the process papers for the execution. Upon seeing that there was never any process, he ordered the prisoners to be loaded onto a truck and taken to a processing center at a nearby army headquarters. Dominique said that being loaded on a truck and transported for a few hours although he was very weak from lack of food and being beaten up was better than the alternative. During the transport American fighter planes had buzzed the truck and the driver stopped and abandoned the truck. Dominique knew that if he stayed on the truck that he would be killed so he and the other prisoners managed to roll themselves off the truck, hit theground and roll away.

A few seconds later, the truck was bombed. Apparently he was still traumatized from that incident. Another time I had noticed four, five scars on his back and one day I asked him what that was about. He said that, at the war's end, he was now a soldier and one of his duties was to canvas German villages for any soldiers or citizens who were resisting the surrender. As he was patrolling with another fellow French soldier, they came upon a bombed house where a teenage German boy charged them with a grenade and blew himself up and killed the French soldier that had been in front of him. Dominique suffered shrapnel wounds in his back. I grew to have incredible respect for him the more time we spent together.

After three days of training we had a grand opening with guests from local hotel managers, the media and food critics. Everything was on the house and it was a great success. The following day was our official opening and there was an incredible buzz in the dinning room. My first day on the job in 1982 I made a little over one hundred dollars. I was very pleased with myself. Now I had to find a place to live.

I announced to the community of fellow Knowledge practitioners that I needed a place to live and that my needs were simple: a room with either shared or private bathroom.

Within a week, Jenny (not real name), let me know that she had a spare furnished bedroom with a private shower available and on the bus line to the restaurant. A week later I had enough of my own money to pay my rent and moved in with Jenny and her eight-year old daughter. I made enough money after a month at Dominique's that I bought a used Ford Mustang and felt grounded and solid enough to step out into the world.

EPILOGUE

I had a short affair with a hot Cuban lady after leaving the Ashram. I still wasn't ready for a long term committed relationship so I ended it. I also got a job as a massage therapist in a chiropractic office while continuing to work at Dominique's during the tourist season. In due course, I became licensed after six months of massage school. My marriage to the office manager ended after a year and a half when she was three months pregnant and didn't want to be my wife anymore. Although I was there at my son's birth, his mother and I never reconciled. Shortly after his first birthday, I had a sense that my time in Miami was finished so I sent out psychic feelers for my next destination. I was getting a strong pull for the Los Angeles area which I resisted because my last escapade in Southern California was too insane. During this time my sister Huguette, on her way back to California from the East Coast called and asked if she could come by and visit for a few days. It was a delight to see her and I saw that she had changed and become much more centered than she had been ten years earlier. The pull from LA didn't let up but got stronger so I called my other sister, Dianne, who lived in Studio City and told her that I was considering moving to her area and would there be room in her place for me and my son to make the transition. She welcomed me with open arms and at the end of April of 1987 we moved in with her.

I spent time and money in promoting my work as a Thought Transformation Therapist and I think was a bit naïve in the way I marketed myself. After about a month, on Memorial Day weekend, Huguette told me that I needed to get out there and meet people and let them know what I do and suggested that I accompany her at a grand opening of Ulla's Yoga studio in Sherman Oaks. It was also the weekend that my son's mother was visiting him so my two sisters, my son, his mother and I went to the grand opening. When we walked in together I saw a beautiful blonde who seemed quite centered and well dressed talking to someone and I was immediately attracted to her. After the event, I got her phone number and told her about my marital status

ONE MAN'S SEARCH FOR THE DIVINE

and that I wanted to see her. She told me that her first impression of me coming on to her with my son and my wife standing there was less than appealing even though she also felt some attraction. That woman is my wife Joyce and we've been together ever since.

We got married two years later in Las Vegas on our way back from a week long herbal seminar in Utah and again five months later for family and friends. We've been together for twenty-seven years thanks to the work we did with Imago Relationship Therapy shortly after our marriage. We later trained with Harville Hendrix in New York to become certified Imago Therapists and today we work as a couple to help other couples heal their relationships. I never knew that it was possible to love and be loved to the depths that I experience with Joyce. I'm grateful to Harville and to my teacher Prem Rawat, also known as Maharaji, for giving me the tools to find true happiness and intimacy. To this day I continue to practice the Knowledge that he revealed to me and it's been a great source of wisdom, clarity, peace and fulfillment.

André Patenaude lives in Santa Monica with his wife Joyce. He and his wife are Certified Imago Relationship Therapists and help couples create intimate and loving relationships.

Andre Patenaude

ONE MAN'S SEARCH FOR THE DIVINE

Andre Patenaude

CPSIA information can be obtained
at www.ICGtesting.com
Printed in the USA
BVHW051154171222
654411BV00008B/319